THE SEAGI

C000002650

THE SEAGULL HOTEL

1945

TWO YOUNG WOMEN START A NEW ENTERPRISE

IN EXMOUTH

KIRSTINE RICHARDS

YOUCAXTON PUBLICATIONS

OXFORD & SHREWSBURY

ENQUIRIES@YOUCAXTON.CO.UK

Copyright © Nick & Louanne Richards 2016

The copyright holders assert their moral right to
be identified as the owners of this work.

ISBN 978-191117-542-1
Printed and bound in Great Britain.
Published by YouCaxton Publications 2016

All rights reserved. No part of this publication may be reproduced,
stored in a retrieval system, or transmitted in any form or by
any means, electronic, mechanical, photocopying, recording or
otherwise, without the prior permission of the publisher.

This book is sold subject to the condition that it shall not, by way of
trade or otherwise, be lent, resold, hired out or otherwise circulated
without the publisher's prior consent in any form of binding or cover
other than that in which it is published and without a similar condition
including this condition being imposed on the subsequent purchaser.

In memory of our mother, Kirstine, whose generosity, humour and tireless love enabled us to come through the post-war chaos. May her indomitable spirit, which shines through the telling of this tale, be enjoyed by many readers.

Louanne and Nick Richards – 2016

CONTENTS

CHAPTER 1

DECEMBER 1945 – BLEAK PROSPECTS

Two widows, one ancient car, one small pension, two thousand pounds and a little courage; these were the assets. Two widows, four children under five, no degrees, no talents, diplomas or inspiration; these were the deficits.

The year was 1945 and the month December; it was raw, wet and dismal. Gerdy and I stared bleakly at each other, as whatever we considered entailed complicated journeys to ill paid jobs that barely tolerated children. Only the desperate would want to employ young widows with the hazard of sick children at awkward moments. Who could blame them? At this very moment two had streaming colds and the youngest looked suspiciously spotty.

I felt dejected. I had left Gerdy's house in Hertford that morning with high hopes. My father-in-law had arranged an interview with the matron of one of London's largest hospitals. A vast dignified woman rose as I entered her pleasant room overlooking a small courtyard. She was robed in black from head to toe, only relieved by a small white crackling cap perched on iron grey hair.

She looked capable and composed, making me feel frivolous in my high heels and emerald green hat. With kindness she waived aside my lack of diploma in Institutional Management, explaining that she knew I had experience in cooking for numbers. As I was the widow of one of their doctors she was prepared to give me a trial. With clarity and the resignation of one confronted by impossible staff shortages she outlined the work.

'You would be catering for about 250 patients. You would have a staff of about six under you and you would be expected to run two large kitchens and the various offices that go with them, including a special dietetic department. Do you think you could manage this?'

She paused, while the white cap creaked ominously.

With trepidation, which I hoped I hid, I told her that I thought I could.

She looked at my hat doubtfully and I looked at her with equal misgiving. Then I plucked up courage and asked how much I could expect in the way of salary.

'The salary for this post is £326 yearly, less emoluments of course'

I blinked; this was a word I had never met before. It anyway had only half my attention, as I was hastily trying to work out how much £326 would mean weekly.

'Emoluments' she went on, 'Cover the cost of laundry, food and a compulsory savings fund. I think you could be sure of taking home each week just over £4.'

£4! I stared at her blankly. This would hardly cover the wages of a competent nanny, even if we could get one, which I was pretty sure we could not with every available woman in a factory or the Forces. If we were fortunate enough to find such a person, she would certainly want help with the cooking and housework if she was going to be able to give the children proper attention. Then there would be rent, rates, gas, electricity, fuel, food and clothes. Even if Gerdy found a job at £4 a week and we added my £5 war widow's pension, it was clear that at this rate we should never be able to manage. I stared at her with an expressionless face, wild thoughts churning; angry and rebellious thoughts. But I could see it would be quite useless for me to express them to this kindly and dignified woman, who probably earned little more herself. Useless for me to point out that the work she outlined entailed great responsibility and skill. It was no wonder that hospital catering was so severely criticized, if this was the rate of pay for such an arduous and complicated job.

In that one short conversation I became an ardent post suffragette. What do widows do, I pondered. How do they manage? Who employs them and how do they live? Do they have to give up any hope of keeping a home together?

I remembered with distaste the horrible school where I had been working when I heard of Gerry's death. I thought of the sanctimonious hypocrisy of the headmistress and her sycophantic assistant; the helplessness of those who were in their power for reasons of age or frailty. I recalled the horror, which had swept over me when they suggested that I make my home in the school; they in return educating my children. I could still see the calculating greedy look lying behind their superficial sympathy. I would be a good bargain that 'look' told me, with my capacity for hard work and my skill as a cook. Once they got their hands on my children I would be trapped, too exhausted to break free and look for other work and too cowed to fight for my children's freedom of mind and spirit. Already they had two such mothers on their staff; exploited and blackmailed under cover of sweet concern and their children used as subtle ransom. The discomfort of that place was something I would never forget. The stuffy dismal schoolroom which was the staff sitting room, the hard upright chairs, the dying embers of the fire, the unfilled coal bucket and almost worse than anything, the 15 watt light bulb that made reading or sewing impossible.

Was this all that Gerdy and I could expect from life? Would we have to become humble and bitter as we meekly railed against our fate?

Gerdy was in an even more precarious position than I, as she had no pension. For some obscure reason known only to her now dead husband, he had not believed in insurance, so she had no capital. Fabian had not joined up with all his friends at the beginning of the war, feeling that as a South African married to a German he was in a position to stand on one side and see things objectively. This grew harder for him as the war became more and more bloody and as daily we were bombarded with stories of Nazi atrocities. From being loftily on the defensive and blatantly pacifist, he gradually became quiet and withdrawn, working with fanatical zeal among the sick of Hertford and devoting the rest of his time to his little family. When the bombing became bad he was out night after night with his ambulance unit, working with heroism. It was not surprising that when a patch on one lung was discovered, he had no strength left to fight it and live. Within three weeks of being admitted to hospital he was dead, leaving Gerdy shattered with shock. His isolation from most of his friends had inevitably drawn them very close. I had always felt this to be one of the happiest unions in the deepest sense. Although I found his pacifist views exceedingly irritating, this had in no way affected my admiration for Fabian, as a husband, father and a doctor.

I had loved Gerdy from the first moment we met in Honiton eight years before, when she was a shy sixteen and I, a hesitant twenty one year old. I thought her the most exquisite thing I had ever seen; slender, fair, bronzed and with that rare delicacy often found in Nordic women. She had a clear intelligence and tremendous charm. She had the charm of the continental woman who was completely sure of her value as a woman. To me and to most of my friends, she epitomized glamour. Her father had held a big position in Germany, as Vice President of the Chamber of Commerce. Having seen the war clouds gathering long before most, he had bundled both his lovely daughters out of Germany, fearing they might be caught up in the Nazi machine, which looked as though it might engulf the whole of Europe. Both had married on the eve of war; Gerdy in England and Christel in Brazil.

Gerry and Fabian had been medical students together at St Bartholomew's Hospital. We had met them when they were camping in Cornwall. We became engaged within a week of each other, were married within a fortnight during the Munich crisis. Gerry was killed in Burma on January 23rd 1945, Fabian died two weeks later. We both had two children and everything pointed to our clinging together at this critical time.

Being equally frightened of the future and equally bereft and dazed, it was unnecessary for us to dwell on our grief. It was, as it was, and we would have to cope as best we could. Gerdy couldn't return to her home in Germany, as her parents had lost everything during the war. I had no home I could go to either, so we clung to each other and took comfort from our mutual sorrow. From totally different backgrounds, we had discovered a deep understanding.

After the interview at the hospital I trailed home thoroughly dispirited. We now sat considering and rejecting one suggestion after the other.

'How about... mmm. No that wouldn't do.' 'I wonder if... No, that's not really a feasible idea'

'Perhaps we should... No, that wouldn't work'

'Gerdy:' I said reflectively, 'It's no good, we must do something constructive.' 'How about my going down to Exeter tomorrow, to see my old bank manager? He used to be very kind and he might have a brain wave. When I saw the trustees a few weeks ago they told me they would help in every possible way. They might be able to think of something sensible. If you could cope with the children for a few days, I'll see what he says and come back as quickly as possible.'

I discovered that my old bank manager was dead, killed by a stray bomb in 1942, but his successor, Mr. Gliddon, was charming. A spry, eager, thin man with imaginative eyes behind rimless spectacles and a friendly interested manner. He listened to my story quietly, grasping with refreshing realism the essential details. When I had finished he thought for a few seconds, checked again on the number and ages of the children; mourned a little sadly over the lack of pension for Gerdy and then sank into silence whilst balancing his pen on the palm of his hand.

At last he murmured, 'I think we should have Mr. Bodmin in on this. He is one of the trustees. I believe you met him a few weeks ago? His advice is always sound.'

He gave me a reassuring smile as he pressed a small bell on his desk, while once more sinking into a meditative trance. I found this surprisingly comforting. At last someone was looking at the problem squarely and regarding it as something that had to be solved.

Mr. Bodmin arrived and listened gravely while Mr. Gliddon outlined our difficulties. Then he added,

'I am wondering if the best idea would be for Mrs. Richards to consider opening another business of her own, like her café in Honiton. She made a success of that I'm told.'

Here, he beamed at me while glinting benignly over his spectacles.

'Now she has a double incentive don't you agree?'

I had never thought of Nick and Louanne in this light, but I could see his point.

'Now my dear, do you think you could find suitable premises, and if you found them and the bank lent you the purchase money, would you be able to furnish the place? With what furniture you and Mrs. Ramsay already have and with part of your £2,000 insurance money, do you think it would be possible to equip a place large enough to house all six of you and at the same time leave sufficient room to run a profitable hotel or restaurant? What do you think Mr. Bodmin?' He turned to face him.

I didn't wait to hear Mr. Bodmin's reactions. I was too staggered and far too elated to care what he thought. Of course we could. I didn't hesitate. It was a wonderful idea, almost too good to be true. In one sentence Mr. Gliddon had outlined a plan and a vision that would give us a home, a job and best of all, hope.

'Wait now, Mrs. Richards, remember this is 1945 and the war is barely over. Every single item of furniture, material, sheets, blankets, towels, cutlery and china are all on dockets or coupons or unobtainable. You may be able to get some help, but even if you do, and this is very doubtful, what you get won't be nearly enough to furnish more than a few rooms. Do you realise how difficult it will be; in fact I would go further and I think Mr. Bodmin will agree with me, I think it will be nearly impossible. Do you think you can do the impossible?'

He looked at me quizzically.

'Of course we can, it will be wonderful,' I breathed. What did these difficulties matter? We would manage somehow. Somewhere there must be enough tables, chairs, sheets, blankets. It was just a matter of searching. We'd comb the country until we'd unearthed them. Then we'd paint, upholster, renew, however old and shabby they might be.

I babbled something, but all the time my mind was racing. We would have to find a house and it had better be a hotel, not a restaurant. A hotel sounded a much steadier background for children and it sounded more leisurely for us as well. Where should we start looking?

I thanked them both profusely and could hardly bear to wait whilst they gave me helpful advice, well basted with caution.

I darted ecstatically from the bank. Never before had Exeter looked so beautiful; a lot of it flat, with jagged bits of broken buildings jutting out of the rubble, but to me it was magnificent. The air sparkled, its wintry light tinged with a golden glow, the bombed ruins shining russet red in the vivid sunset. The lacy windows of the bombed cathedral were towering splendidly over the surrounding chaos. I stood for a few moments in the quiet of the shattered chancel, so remote from the noise and bustle of the streets.

God had heard our prayers after all. Through the lively imagination of that eager and sensible bank manager, a miracle had been wrought and six of His flock would be fed. My heart overflowed with gratitude as I rushed for a phone box.

CHAPTER 2

A DERELICT HAVEN

Gerdy must have thought I was demented as I babbled incoherently down the phone. What should we do? Should she bring the children down to my rented Honiton cottage and start the search from there or should I return to her house and look for a place in or near, London?

'No, the sea, it must be near the sea, as it is so good for the children. If we live by the sea we should never have to think of expensive holidays.'

But first we must get rid of these rented houses, so it had better be Gerdy's place. But wait, if we have to equip a hotel wherever it was, surely it would be better to search for furniture near London. There would be much more choice there. Cornwall and Devon had been swept bare by relays of refugees pouring out of the bombed cities.

First we must find a suitable house or hotel then collect as much stuff as we could. Then we could move down to my little house, so that we could superintend the painting and organizing with as little difficulty as possible. What fun it was going to be! At last we had a plan and the awful indecision was over.

We decided that I should start the preliminary search while I was still in Exeter and then, if I found a likely place, Gerdy would have to park the children with a neighbour and rush down to give her approval.

I felt mean having the exciting part to do, but she assured me she would hate having to deal with agents and bank managers, and would far rather stay at home. The children were being good, the neighbours helpful and the spots had disappeared.

That night I pored over a map of Devon. I knew most of the coast was mined and very few beaches were accessible. I had no idea when these would be cleared, if ever. Exmouth seemed to be the most hopeful, with over three miles of sand. A phone call to a friend living there assured me that much of the beach was, as far as she knew, free of mines. There was still a lot of barbed wire and many pill boxes, but certain stretches of the shore were free and more were being cleared every month. She would be delighted to put me up and Jack, her husband, would help in every possible way.

Jack was one of those men who knew everyone, and even better, he seemed to know exactly how to get the best out of them. Everyone liked and trusted him, which was surprising when one knew of his appetite for gossip. He spent a great deal of his time in pubs and at his club, maintaining no doubt with absolute truth, that he did far more business in this way than he ever did in his office. His gossip was completely innocent of malice and he had the uncanny knack of being able to put people in touch with one another at exactly the right moment.

His wife, plump, blonde and motherly, had devoted her whole life to cosseting him. He was her father, brother, husband and infant child all untidily parceled into this exuberant bouncing little man.

Fortunately Jack knew several of the estate agents personally. He sleuthed and badgered them until they disclosed their cherished secrets. He found out which hotel property was about to be de-requisitioned, which would then be up for sale, what state they were in after four years of army occupation, what sort of price they would fetch, how much bomb damage they had suffered and how much Government Grant might be expected. He was wonderful in the information he was able to garner each day.

Every morning we met like conspirators, crouching round a one bar electric fire, for electricity was still severely rationed. This place would be too large, that one too expensive and the other was a ruin. This one would be occupied for the whole of the summer, that one had mysterious strings attached and we must not contemplate the other. And then on the fourth night a miracle happened!

'Come quickly Kirstine, I believe I've found just the place. It's to be de-requisitioned next month. The owner wants to emigrate to Australia, so will accept a reasonable price for a quick sale. It's freezing, so put on another coat and here's a scarf. Now, hurry'.

Out into the crackling cold we went, walking swiftly beside a hushed and tranquil sea. The stars hung huge and glittering against the dense purple sky, whilst a pale moon sailed dignified and aloof through the drifting clouds. Our breath hung on the air like damp lace; my face aching and tingling with excitement and cold. I peered up at a large abandoned house standing alone on a corner, which was staring with unseeing eyes at the glistening sea. Its plaster was broken off in great jagged lumps and the roof had gaping holes. Most of the windows were broken and those on the ground level were closely boarded. Not a crack of light showed anywhere and it looked lonely and forbidding. Then as I watched, a dark silent shape detached itself from the roof, circled the chimney pots and alighted delicately on the tip of the highest gable.

It was a seagull – so beautiful and so graceful, and a symbol of freedom and independence, pulsating with life. I felt it was an omen, for surely this bird more than any other survives against tremendous odds – battered by waves, hurricanes, tempests and then resting on the wind regaining strength, it readies itself to greet another day with its haunting mournful cry.

We would buy this derelict building and make of it a thing of beauty, a home for the children and a source of income for ourselves, as well as a haven for those who needed a temporary resting place. We would call it 'THE SEAGULL' – no matter if the building was almost a wreck.

We would work with the strength of ten men and create out of chaos and desolation something secure, free and strong. The name 'THE SEAGULL' sounded good to me and I felt a faint surge of happiness, the first since Gerry's death.

CHAPTER 3

DOCKETS, RATION CARDS AND TEA COUPONS

Things began to move fast after this. I saw the derelict hotel in daylight. It looked even more forlorn and yet for all its shabbiness it gave an impression of honest dependability and well proportioned beauty. There were hardly any stairs beyond the first landing and no banisters at all. The walls were filthy, paint was non-existent and most of the top floor ceilings were bomb damaged. It had been occupied by Canadians, the Durham Light Infantry, black Americans, and judging by the result, none of them were house-proud. But the position was superb; the rooms light and full of reflections from the sea shimmering and flickering in the frail winter sunshine. Seagulls swooped and dipped across the sky and I knew that however abandoned this house was now, it could never be lonely with so much lively movement all around. There were four floors with seven rooms on each landing. One bathroom and lavatory served the whole house. This was no millionaire's plaything; just a hideous peeling yellowish grey bath, lavatory pan black with age and careless usage and a frayed string hanging dispiritedly from a dripping cistern beside a carefully blacked out window.

The sitting room was beautifully proportioned with three enormous windows reaching from floor to ceiling, and a magnificent view of the bay. The basement was depressingly gloomy with broken doors, windows and sinister cubby holes exuding an all pervading smell of rubber and cats. But it had possibilities with two big rooms opening onto the garden allowing plenty of room for prams and toys.

The entrance hall, redesigned just before the war, was spaciously pleasing with big wide curved doors leading directly on to the road. All the ground floor rooms had doors of light oak and glass, which increased the effect of rippling light. A small room just beside the entrance, panelled throughout in pale oak which was almost invisible under layers of grime and ink stains, would make a splendid office and private sitting room. I longed to attack it there and then with vim and a strong scrubbing brush. I promised myself it would be one of my first jobs.

The property was freehold which pleased Mr. Gliddon who considered £5,500 not too high a price.

Gerdy arrived, dazzled Mr. Gliddon, and as excited as I, approved of The Seagull. She had brought with her wonderful news. Her sister in Brazil had cabled offering to lend her £2,000. This meant that we should not have to borrow the full £5,500 from the bank, thus lightening our load considerably. She was now on an equal footing with me, I knew this meant a great deal to her.

We returned to Hertford together the next day, agog to start furniture hunting, leaving the agent to fix details of the sale with our lawyer. As soon as we arrived we drew up long lists of the absolute necessities. Then armed with these, we tackled the Ministry of Labour, confident that when they knew of our need we should be issued with sheets of dockets and coupons, perhaps their good wishes as well. A bored, middle aged woman with greasy hair plastered down on a flat broad head looked at us stonily while remaining unmoved by our story.

'I'm afraid you've come to the wrong place,' she told us. 'We cannot help you. We deal only with lost coupons, expectant mothers and new born babies. Perhaps the Ministry of Supply can assist' and she shooed us away, indignant that we should have wasted her time.

'Poor babies' we commented as we stood uncertainly on the steps outside.

In the Ministry of Supply a wispy woman with incredulous eyebrows greeted us warily.

'Oh no ladies' she snapped, 'We don't deal with anything of this order'. Then hobbling away on thin matchstick legs, her back expressing profound disapproval, she shot at us over her hunched shoulder, 'Try Agriculture and Fisheries.'

'She must be mad,' we muttered as feeling we were getting hopelessly off our track, we approached Agriculture and Fisheries. They too, were unable to help, suggesting we should approach the Hotels' Association. This we did but it seemed that unless one had been an hotelier before the war, and lost everything in a blitz, there was no chance of getting even one coupon or docket. In vain we pointed out to all these departments that we had to make a living in order to live; that four tiny children made ordinary jobs quite impossible and were anyway so badly paid we should starve. Running a business under one's own roof would appear to be the only practical way of managing. But in order to do this we would have to have proper equipment. Without those vital dockets we were unable to buy even a teaspoon. Surely it was better for widows to become self-supporting, work hard and build up some sort of security for themselves and their children.

But the various Ministries weren't remotely interested. We gained the impression that they found us unreasonable and that if we looked carefully enough there was sure to be a department that dealt with this kind of aggravating problem. They were sure that somewhere there must be a slot for us, which would leave them in peace, but just at the moment they couldn't bring it to mind.

'Now ladies, please leave us – we have work to do.'

We were stumped. We didn't dare write to Mr. Gliddon who had warned us that this could happen. I had given him my word that we could furnish the place. I felt I couldn't admit failure at this, our very first hurdle. Tired and snappy we trudged along the crowded streets. It had been dispiriting facing rejection after starting out with such high hopes. We had been so sure we would be encouraged, even praised for our enterprise.

'I can't understand zees people,' Gerdy complained.

'Always taking offence, so unhelpful and so stupid.'

'They are not like that in Scotland' I protested, ever anxious to protect my native heath. 'They'd help us up there.'

'Well we're not in Scotland, we are here in bloody London. My feet hurt, my head aches. That bank man was right – ve vill never be able to furnish that enormous place.' She looked close to tears, sombre green eyes misting, tender lips quivering.

'We will Gerdy. I know we will. It's just a matter of making a start.' But I was none too sure. Frightened and disheartened we trailed back to Hertford in a frozen silence of despair.

Chapter 4

January 1946 – Shady Dealings

Gerdy's neighbour, who had been so kind in caring for the children on several occasions, mentioned a street market in a nearby town.

'Every Saturday' she told us, 'There are masses of stalls. One of my friends got a beautiful pair of Irish linen sheets there a few weeks ago. Of course you mustn't mention this to anyone as it isn't altogether legal, but if one of you care to come with me next Saturday I could introduce you to my friend. If she likes you she might be willing to show you the ropes?' She looked at us questioningly.

Gerdy was doubtful. A law abiding person through having spent her childhood in Germany under Hitler's regime, she was unsure of her position in Britain and without Fabian's protection felt doubly vulnerable. I examined my conscience finding it sanguine. Certainly I never before had felt the need of the black market; things had been tough during the war but one managed. But this was a different problem. We could not manage without help and if the Government weren't prepared to deal with us sensibly when we asked for assistance in a straightforward way, then we must take our chance along with everyone else.

We all had to pay for our stupidity so why not the Government who were showing singular idiocy. I suppose this is the argument used by every law breaker, but I felt we had a better case than most. I also liked the added spice of danger.

Mrs. Vickery took me to the market. There we met her friend in a small over-heated crowded café. Mrs. Marks, a quiet nervous woman scrutinised me guardedly over a cup of something vaguely resembling coffee, whilst Mrs. Vickery and I talked of bomb damage, children and the scarcity of meat. I must have passed some mysterious test for she leant forward and in a low whisper breathed, 'Av you ever done this afore?'

'No, I'm afraid not,' I lowered my voice to match hers.

'Well now you as to be careful and keep yer eyes skint. You never knows oos scoutin arand. There's some I could tell you abart,' she shot a disapproving look at three women innocently drinking tea at the next table.

'There's some that can't mind their own business. Now ducks follow me and do as I do and don't you talk to no one.'

She gave me a shove and led the way to join a huddle of women clustered round the stalls.

The market was in full swing, jostling the sullen day with vibrant energy. Throngs of ruddy faced men and women shoved, pushed, argued, laughed and gossiped. Their children, darting underfoot while giggling and joking, were reprimanded, spanked, shaken, slapped, noses blown, then wriggled away ready to get into the same mischief all over again.

Endless stories were told and retold. A shabby respectable rollicking gaiety prevailed; quite new to me, who was more used to orderly queues in shelf-bare Devon shops.

Stall holders shouted demonstrating their wares, teasing the young girls, poking friendly insults at the bolder women, deferring to the elderly prim housewives bent on more serious business.

One vendor tossed plates with nerve wracking dexterity, another snapped suspenders demonstrating their flexibility. Mounds of vegetables jostled with a few crinkled apples. I caught a glimpse of contraband bananas and oranges being thrust surreptitiously into baskets. Straw blew around untidy piles of cartons and boxes spilling their debris, as the icy January wind reddened cheeks and rattled awnings. One man lost his hat, a girl's skirt blew over her head. The crowd roared with delight; hardship forgotten for a moment in the comedy of living.

'That's David,' whispered Mrs. Marks as we pushed our way through. I watched with interest as a square solid man extolled the charms of a pair of long-legged pink woollen knickers. A hirsute man with a chin the colour and texture of gritty mussels and bare arms thickly coated with a curly black mat. His swift snapping eyes were brown and shrewd. He wore his cap pushed well back, exposing a cow's-lick of blue black oily hair. I admired the almost lyrical quality of his cockney as he pointed out the durability, shape, colour and design of this delectable female article.

'Ere you are ladies – you won't find better, strite from the makers these knickers are. See. Warm, comfortable, strong.' He waved them energetically above his head. 'Na. 0o will make me an offer? Two pairs for the price of one, and you'll never regret it. Warm, cosy, the colour's fast. See ere,' and he tossed them in the air.

I noticed an enormous pear shaped man sitting on an inadequate stool placed beside the stall. I could see he shared my admiration of David. As well as being a genius in this man's sardonic eyes, he was quite obviously his son. He had the same sturdy build and same pronounced nose. As I watched I saw a woman detach herself from the group, mouthing something in David's direction as she edged herself over to the seated man. Without altering his flow of language by one syllable, David flickered an eyelid in his father's direction. The fat man twitched one ear towards the vegetable stall, which lay alongside David's stall. The woman, as she passed the seated man, dropped something white on to his vast lap. In a flash it disappeared. By this time she was thoughtfully fingering a pile of cabbages, then casually, as though she had just put it down in order to prod the vegetables, she picked up a large brown paper parcel, which had mysteriously appeared by her side. She walked slowly away. All had happened in a few seconds. I was sure no one else had noticed this manoeuvre. I drifted along behind her, mesmerised by her movements. I watched as she met a friend and surreptitiously drew aside one corner of the paper. With amazement I saw what looked like a pure white woolly blanket. Impossible! New blankets had been off the market for the last five years. All one could get now were hideous dark grey and red striped horse rugs, which weighed a ton and smelt of wet socks. But it certainly looked like a blanket.

Deeply impressed I rejoined Mrs. Marks. So this was 'THE BLACK MARKET'. That elusive, subtle, shifting crime of which everyone had heard, but with which no one I knew had ever come in direct contact. I felt stimulated, and mustering every ounce of gangster charm waited for my meeting with David.

Mrs. Marks at last pushed me forward hissing, 'My friend here would like a pair of nylons luv. Any luck?' She gave him a prim leer.

David shut one expressive eye, groped under the stall, and then shoved a pair of these unheard of luxuries into my willing hand. I was overwhelmed with gratitude. Stammering my thanks, whilst my new friend told David in a breathy whisper of our hotel in Devon, our husband's deaths and our difficulty with dockets and coupons. David listened intently, murmuring about 'times being hard ducks.'

'You don't want to worry with they stoopid bits of paper,' giving me shrewd sidelong looks. Then out of the corner of his stubbly mouth he muttered, 'Come next week darlin and bring the lolly.'

'How much shall I bring,' I stuttered, wild with excitement. 'A hundred nicker,' he said. 'Got a car?' I nodded. 'But watch it darlin. Back your car against Charlie's veg there, mind there ain't no coppers flat footing around.'

'I'll be careful,' I whispered, feeling as though I was the heroine of a David Lean film.

I must practise talking out of the side of my mouth. It was not easy. It seemed such a strange way to do one's shopping. I hadn't told David what I wanted to buy, David had given me no indication of what he had to sell, but when you have nothing and need everything, anything would be wonderful. I floated home to Gerdy to tell her of my success.

The following Saturday I packed all four children into the car feeling they would lend an air of innocence to the whole affair, leaving Gerdy clearing spaces in her airing cupboard ready for the loot. We drove off in high spirits the children shrieking at the tops of their exceedingly tough lungs.

Nick was aged 5, blonde, dreamy, affectionate, imaginative and unpredictable. A mysterious child, not unlike a bottle of homemade ginger pop; ready to fizz over the edge or blow his cork with an unexpected bang. But today the cork was securely fixed and all was exuberant calm. Taking him into bed for a cuddle was like trying to embrace a collection of garden tools; all bones, elbows, notches and sudden jerks.

Louanne was aged 3½, a compact little thing with fair skin, straight copper gold hair, large thoughtful grey eyes; dignified and sensible in her requests, and adamant if they were not met. Only reason could deflect her from her chosen course; then only if your reason was a better one than hers. It seldom was. Not for her the evasive reply or absent minded 'because I say so'. Rosily rounded like a golden marigold I found her utterly enchanting and a little unnerving.

Christel was a month younger than Lu. She was slow and dreamy like Nick, but very observant and tending to drift through life like a blown leaf; all eyes, ears, hesitations and sudden stops. Smooth pale brown hair that straggled into turquoise blue eyes fringed with long black curly lashes. An appealing, though maddening child who was always in need of prodding.

Adrian, a bouncing twenty months; plump like a freshly baked cottage loaf, already bursting with charm and rollicking good humour. He and Lu were natural affinities, just as Nick and Christel gravitated to one another. All were protective of Adrian who needed protection least of all.

'Now children, listen carefully, this is very important. Nick take that dinky toy off Adrian's head, Lu do stop hugging him like that. He can't breathe. Christel are you listening? Now I want you all to sit very still, be very quiet. Nick please watch out carefully and tell me if you see a policeman.'

Hoping this wasn't the beginning of a life of crime for them, I backed the car against the vegetable stall as instructed. David didn't appear to have noticed me and went on waving a vast pair of corsets above his head, while extolling their charms. I drifted in amongst the crowd, caught a swift blink from David evenly divided between myself and fat father who was still sitting on his inadequate stool. He was without doubt the ugliest man I had ever seen, with a tiny head perched on sloping shoulders which descended untidily into the folds and contours of an enormous paunch. His behind was vast and overlapping the stool by several feet. He stared straight through me and then one eyelid dropped. Was this a cue? Another blink; it must be! I edged my way forward until we almost touched. There was still no sign of recognition as I dropped my carefully prepared envelope on to his solid lap. Without moving a muscle it vanished. Was he going to count the £100? What should I do now? I gazed at Pa. One eyelash quivered in the direction of the vegetable stall.

A small wizened man with black-currant eyes sidled up to me muttering, 'Open the boot or do you want the bits inside lidy? All's clear but look sharp.' His eyes darted in all directions.

I caught sight of four pairs of round eyes peering out of the car. Lu's faintly suspicious, Christel's scenting mischief, Nick's entranced, Adrian frankly amused. I hastily opened the door and we stuffed three large lumpy parcels under the children who rose by several surprised inches.

'Look sharp lidy, copper coming this way.' Never before had I felt so frightened.

Charlie thrust four bananas into the children's eager outstretched hands (the first they'd ever seen) causing much mystified speculation. I leapt into the driving seat and amidst excited shrieks from Nick of, 'Mummy, mummy, I can see a policeman. You told me to tell you if I saw a policeman. I can see one now. Look, look.'

We whizzed out of the market square. As we passed the policeman he gave the children a beaming smile. Little did he know!

What had we got? Had we been duped? Would we find rubbish when we opened the bundles? They had felt solid, heavy, so they could be sheets. How wonderful if they were! I couldn't get home fast enough and as we swung into Gerdy's road I could see her peering anxiously from an upstairs window. She darted down as we drew up and together we hauled the packages into the hall. The children, still clutching the bananas, gathered round as we dragged off the wrappings. The first contained a bale of beautiful beech brown brocade. It could easily have been hideous, but by some miracle it was quite the prettiest material we had seen in years. There were yards and yards of it, so perhaps there would be enough to make curtains for those enormous dining room windows and maybe sufficient left over to upholster chairs – that's if we found any chairs. The second bundle contained six pairs of Irish linen sheets and twelve pillow cases with hem stitched edges. The third bundle had four fleecy white blankets! We almost wept with gratitude. David had done us proud. It was a beginning; with David behind us we could face the nightmare task that lay ahead.

We could hold heads high when next we met Mr. Gliddon, for by now we were beginning to appreciate the courage he had shown in backing us.

We stowed the loot away, walking on air for the rest of the day. The children, after the excitement of the parcels, settled down to the serious business of how to deal with bananas. I don't know what Adrian expected but it wasn't what he got. He took one experimental bite then spat it out with an indignant yell, much to the delight of the others who gobbled up his share with alacrity.

Every Saturday for many weeks I followed the same routine. Gerdy never got used to the idea, always nervously looking for lurking policemen when we reached home, but she knew it was the only way, bravely hiding her unease in front of the children.

At the market we never exchanged more than a few words, father never counted the money and I never questioned what David produced. Each week there would be bundles of things which were absolutely vital; sometimes material, usually sheets and towels, occasionally blankets. On one special occasion there were a dozen quilts, heavy and crude, but they were warm, far better than anything we ever saw in the shops. Every week amidst squeals of delight the children were given fruit. This of course became the outing of the week for them.

On week days we scoured the country for second-hand furniture. We found it useless to come within twenty miles of London, as the prices soared the nearer we were to the centre of the city. The poorer districts were best and here we trudged in and out of shop after shop. In one we had a stroke of luck. Chairs were hard to come by, what few there were very expensive. Whilst prowling around a grubby second hand mart, we came upon a large pile of ordinary Victorian chairs; some quite pleasing with carved frames and others perfectly plain. The ancient man who was in charge of the store was vague. When we asked the price he seemed baffled. He'd probably been nabbed to mind the shop whilst the owner popped out for a quick one. He pondered, and then hesitatingly suggested 10 shillings. We thought this pretty good and asked,

'How much if we took the lot?' He thought again then mumbled, 'Mmm I should say about 5 shillings.' This really was a bargain, as they appeared to be in good shape.

We climbed on to the pile, passing them down one by one, eliminating those that were cracked. In this way we managed to collect 50. The seats were a ruin, but we felt reasonably sure that if re-webbed, re-stuffed, then covered with the new brocade, they would look fine. The vague little man hopped around bewildered, wondering no doubt whether he was going to get praised when the owner returned, for selling so many so fast, or scolded for selling so cheap.

Gradually we collected a chest of drawers here, a cupboard there, all left to be collected on some distant day. Tables were our best buy; solid mahogany, walnut, rosewood and round, square or oval, for sometimes as little as £5. No one, it seemed, wanted Victoriana in 1946.

Beds were out greatest worry. We travelled miles, shamelessly borrowing petrol coupons, but never could we find beds. Gradually everyone heard of the search and we'd get urgent messages to go here, there and everywhere. Always when we got to wherever it was, the bed was either sold or it was filthy and exuding stuffing and undreamt of horrors. Desperate as we were we could not bring ourselves to touch or far less buy them.

Then on one particularly cold March day we saw a hopeful looking shop with well lighted windows and an air of businesslike bustle. Parking the car on a nearby bomb site, we battled our way through an evil sleeting wind into the warmth of the shop. A supercilious salesman gave us a chilly look as we dragged our straggling collection of progeny through the door. Christel, as usual, staring so hard she got wedged, Nick indignant because he hadn't been allowed to bring in all his dinky cars. Gerdy and I stopped dead. There, right in front of us, was a brand new divan. We swooped and Gerdy sat down firmly, looking as though she was prepared to sit there for the rest of time. I spotted another in a far corner.

'Quickly Lu,' I cried, 'Go and sit on that bed and don't move darling.'

As our eyes became accustomed to the dazzle of the lighted shop we saw there were beds everywhere; beautiful new bouncing divans in clear exciting colours. Quickly we plonked a child on each one and waited patiently until one of the lofty salesmen deigned to notice us. At last one, kinder than the rest, came over and listened patiently to our babbling. He wasn't to know that to us he represented Houdini and Merlin rolled into one.

Yes, they had plenty of beds. Of course they all had mattresses. Forty? Yes, he thought he could manage that number. Coupons dockets? Quite unnecessary and he looked pained as though we had used a dirty word.

Did they have any cots? Yes, he thought they had. With mattresses? Of course. This was obviously a fantasy and we should wake up. But no, gradually it became apparent that here we should find most of the things we needed so badly. Our order became bigger and bigger. From being regarded as a bunch of vagrants, we became valued customers. By now we had collected several eager salesmen, who pressed us to look at this and consider that. Periodically one of us had to rush out into the piercing wind to wrestle on the bomb site with buttons and zips whilst one or other of the children answered the call of nature, but this was tactfully ignored by the now enthusiastic retinue.

At last, feeling we had brought as much as we dared, a vast bill was totted up. By now, we were sitting in state in the manager's private office, being plied with cups of tea and many compliments. Gerdy gave the bill one horrified look and handed it on to me. £689! Never before had I written such a cheque. Silently praying that Mr. Gliddon would honour it, I wrote the date. I got as far as March 19th when the door was flung open and there stood Nick with a flaming, indignant face, 'Mummy, Lulu's wet her pants, and it's all your fault for buying so many beds.'

There was a quiet hush whilst I wrote out the rest of the cheque. The interchange of silent looks told us that we were not of the stuff of which big buyers are made. Nevertheless, we had our beds.

CHAPTER 5

JUNE 1946 – DESPERATE MEASURES

I wonder why women are always in a hurry and men seldom seem infected by this desperate urge to get things done. Is it because of the pressure of the thousand and one little jobs that lie at our heels, so we feel we must rush through every task at break-neck speed in order to tackle the next one, or is it that we are just naturally more impatient? If any of my women friends want a piano or cupboard moved they are in an agony of impatience until the job is done, while brothers, husbands and fathers procrastinate for weeks in dignified calm.

Despite phone calls, letters and several visits, nothing had moved in Exmouth. We felt it imperative that we should be there ourselves to speed things up. Even the knowledgeable Jack had begun to look grave having lost his grip on his friend the agent.

'Don't worry,' we were told repeatedly. 'Derequisitioning is slow and complicated.'

It certainly was. It looked as though we should end up with a stack of furniture and nowhere to put it.

It was early July before we finally left Hertford feeling confident we had bought all we could. In our innocence we imagined that it would be a few months before we could open 'The Seagull'. We should be well established before Christmas, we told ourselves. There must be many people coming out of the forces just longing for the kind of family festivities we were prepared to provide.

We took a fond farewell of our friends in the market, David wishing us good luck, offering to send anything we might need. He thrust a pair of blue satin cami-knickers at me as a parting gift. Father pear almost smiled as he handed the children a carton of cherries. Even Charlie popped a cabbage in my hands as he stowed the last bundle in the boot. We felt quite sentimental. I vowed that if ever there was another war I should make straight for the nearest market, where life goes on much the same, where no one worries too much about ethics, principles, queues or fair play, and where ordinary human kindness takes over, making daily living possible and reasonable.

On our first visit to Exmouth we realised with a nasty jolt that derequisitioning did indeed take time. As no one person accepts responsibility, no one person can be cajoled or intimidated.

The agent, earnest and conscientious, was deeply impressed by protocol. He wore a bright red wig. We could understand the need for a wig, but were baffled by the colour which seemed to defeat its own purpose. He advised patience, adding for good measure;

'All will be resolved in time.'

Our lawyer, an old friend of many years standing, was urbane, shrewd and wise and he advised caution. What solicitor advises anything else? He came down from Birmingham, stood us a delicious lunch at the Royal Clarence in Cathedral Square, charmed us with kindness and compliments, and retired to oblivion in the Midlands for the next four months.

Hopping with impatience we decided to interest a builder so that the moment the hotel was in our hands he could rush in with an army of enthusiastic painters, carpenters and bricklayers. The agent had advised us to go to a certain Mr. Fynn, who recently demobbed, was full of new ideas. We found a plump easygoing chap who assured us he had plenty of men. Once we got the 'PERMIT' he would start work. Permit? What was this? Who applied for it, where was it issued? He did it seemed, and Exeter dished out permits.

'Well then Mr. Fynn, do go ahead and apply.'

But this he told us he was unable to do until the hotel was in our name. Back we went to the agent.

'Have patience dear ladies, these things cannot be hurried. All will resolve itself in time,' and he gave his wig a little pat.

Six weeks later, after much agitation on our part, we signed the lease. At last The Seagull was ours. Sizzling with excitement, we hammered on Mr. Fynn's door.

'Splendid, splendid, I'll apply right away. Now just leave everything to me. In no time at all I shall have my men down there and we shall start work.' He gave Gerdy an admiring look. I had noticed that he responded to Gerdy's beauty with more alacrity that to my brisker charms. We decided she should be used to put on pressure when things slowed up.

'What a wonderful man,' we assured each other. 'So keen, calm and sensible, so well aware of the need for speed.'

Another two weeks and we were back on his doorstep. 'No', he hadn't got the permit yet. There was a small delay. Nothing serious but we must have patience.

'I think he's doing his best don't you?' we asked each other doubtfully.

At the beginning of August we tried again. 'No, it hasn't arrived yet, but they've promised faithfully it will be sent within a couple of days'.

'I don't think that man has any idea of hurrying', we muttered by now exasperated.

A week later we rang to ask where this Ministry was, who we should see. We were by now determined to take action ourselves.

'Oh,' said Mr. Fynn, 'There's no need for you to do that. I'm doing everything possible. We don't want to make them angry do we?'

We told him this might not be a bad idea. If we were continually on their doorstep, they might give us the wretched thing in order to get rid of us. Mr. Fynn didn't agree.

'It's most unethical. They would only get annoyed and put your claim at the bottom of the pile. Remember there are many other people with claims as well as yourselves. You leave this to me. I shan't let you down.'

By the end of August we were frightened and very angry. Mr. Gliddon was asking awkward questions and we were in a difficult position financially. The Royal Medical Benevolent Society had granted Gerdy a small sum each week for six months after Fabian's death, but this had now come to an end. My pension of £5 a week barely met our expenses however careful we were, and the small amount of money we had saved was now at an end. We dared not borrow from the bank for personal expenses, yet somehow we had to live. Mr. Gliddon couldn't understand why the builders weren't well on the way to completing the alterations. He told us something must be done, but what? He said he knew of a builder who guaranteed that he could start work right away.

But here we discovered a stumbling block which was explained to us by the now offended Mr. Fynn. The builder who applied for the permit must do the work. It could on no account be transferred. Meanwhile we had been hearing disquieting stories about Mr. Fynn, and were uneasy about placing ourselves in his lackadaisical hands. It wasn't a small job. The estimate came to just over £1,500 and he could get up to any number of tricks with so much at stake. We had heard that some builders could and did, accept a variety of jobs and then play this delaying game until they were in a position to start work many months later. By moving their men from job to job, they could keep several pots on the boil. Banks were more likely to lend money if they could show they had several jobs in hand. This was, we were sure, Mr. Fynn's system. Could it be that he had already acquired the permit as security for a bank loan?

Distrusting Mr. Fynn, and being so short of money, it would be madness to embark on many months of extensive alterations in his slippery care. By now we hated his soapy smarmy manner, but swallowing our dislike we asked, as politely as possible, whether we could see this precious document which had caused so much trouble. He rummaged about in his desk producing a small bit of white paper. What a fuss for such an insignificant little thing. I gave Gerdy a warning glance. As he held it out I snatched it from his hand and bolted for the door.

He gasped and shouted, 'You can't do this – it isn't legal.'

I caught a glimpse of Gerdy's ashen face as I whizzed by.

'I'll have the law on you for this!' he yelled.

'Oh no you won't,' I yelped as I nipped through the door. 'There are far too many things you want to keep hidden.'

This was a long shot, but it must have found its mark, for we never heard another word from Mr. Fynn.

Our new builder, Mr. White, chuckled wickedly when we told him of our piracy. We wondered nervously if he might refuse to handle such an unorthodox permit, but he was obviously hugely pleased, having no scruples about builders' etiquette. Within a week he had twenty men on the job. At last things were underway.

Chapter 6

September 1946 – Constant Preparations

In eight short months we had come a long way. From being respectable doctors' wives, upright mothers, full of splendid principles, absolutely sure of the difference between right and wrong, here we were with a house full of black market contraband, a debt running into thousands mounting daily, and the stain of theft and blackmail on our conscience.

Where would it all end I wondered? I couldn't include Gerdy for she had resisted all the way, only falling in with my plans because there seemed no alternative. She got no pleasure out of it. I, on the other hand, got quite a kick out of each successful encounter.

Perhaps, when everything was organised with the hotel running smoothly, I should be able to return to my original high standards. May be this downfall was temporary and the rot which had set in might drop off leaving me pure and shining, morally above censure. I felt I ought to ask God to help me fight temptation, but knew at this point, such a step would be sheer hypocrisy as I had every intention of continuing with criminal activities until we were firmly on our feet.

In early September we brought all the furniture we had collected down from London, stacking it in two of the largest rooms.

We ourselves had fitted fairly comfortably into my tiny house in Honiton where we had good friends who cared for the children occasionally. Honiton was also the hometown of my eccentric mother, an indomitable, restless woman, with a lofty disdain for the conventional. She held strong views, particularly on religious matters, and had little tact. Though an ardent Christian Scientist she patronised all denominations in turn and such was the force of her personality that the various priests and ministers found themselves entangled in complicated theological discussions in which they were invariably defeated. She was way ahead of her time in terms for the need for unity between the churches.

My mother had opposed our plans vigorously.

'Whatever do you want to run a hotel for?' she demanded incredulously.

'We need to eat,' I answered coldly. 'How can we feed all these children without any money? We can't get money if we don't work and no one will give us work because we have children.'

'Money, money,' she replied with barbed animosity. 'You've got your pension. You've no need to go running hotels.' She gave me an indignant stare; making hotels sound like wild bohemian nightclubs.

'The children need you at home with them. A hotel is no place for little children. They need the undivided attention of their mother.'

At this her look became falsely sentimental. False for I knew she had never relished motherhood all that much herself.

'But mother, do please be sensible. How can six of us manage on £5 a week?'

'I do' thundered my mother. 'I live on a lot less than that.'

My mind flew to her endless bowls of lumpy porridge, which she assured us were nourishing and, as an afterthought, cheap.

'But mother you don't have to pay rent. Your house is your own. I have to pay £2 a week for mine and that leaves £3 to cover food, rates, gas, electricity, clothes, toothpaste for all of us.' 'You have no faith,' she answered haughtily. 'No faith at all. Consider the lilies of the field. The Good Lord will provide if you have faith.' She stalked off before I could retort acidly. 'Well the Good Lord has had plenty of time and so far hasn't come up with a better idea.'

But she was out of earshot. However, there was one good thing about my mother, she never bore a grudge and always took the children off our hands when we were extra busy.

She adored Nick who was enchanted by his entertaining Granny. His vivid imagination pleased her, as they met in an unspoken world of fantasy. They would trudge off happily together in search of other people's apples, eggs or firewood, usually returning with a pram load of treasures; the origin of which I did not enquire into too deeply. She had almost no sense of property, being overjoyed to share her house, food or possessions with any passing wayfarer; quite unable to understand the more normal attitude of 'What's mine is my own.' This she called un-Christian and became unpopular in so doing.

Lu was puzzled by Granny's swift changes of mood, finding them inexplicable. My mother who could never meet reason with reason found Lu equally baffling.

Christel and Adrian accepted her like the weather; a bit blustery, sometimes tempestuous. But she came and went and with any luck might leave a trail of apples or sweeties in her stormy wake. Occasionally we despatched the children to my mother for a picnic. Adrian would be pushed erratically in his pram by the girls, precariously balanced on bags of buns and pints of milk. They usually ended up in some outlying church, no doubt bewildering many a quiet vicar. This gave us time to catch up on curtain making, for with fifteen bedrooms and three large reception rooms to equip, we had much to do. If we measured and cut without the hazard of children clambering around, chewing up pins, randomly reckless with scissors, then the actual stitching could be done at any time.

If we had not been so harassed for both money and time I think this could have been called a happy interlude. We were busy and hopeful. We felt sure we could make a success of the hotel, but always we had the nagging feeling that we were squandering time and always I felt guilty because we were never able to give the children as much attention as they needed. We were realising fast that when children lose their fathers they lose their mothers as well.

In exchange they get a distracted automaton with only half her mind on the job of mothering.

Why does everyone conspire to make me feel so guilty I wondered sadly, as if one wasn't guilty enough already in enjoying this challenge. If I'd listened to all the advice, which had poured in from every side, I should be sitting in genteel solitude waiting for some de-mobbed serviceman to offer his hand in marriage.

I looked at Gerdy, head bent over her sewing, her soft cheek caught in the golden glow of a sudden shaft of sunlight and her fair hair falling like a screen masking her eyes. Her inscrutable face told me nothing. I could not be certain of what she really felt about this venture. She acquiesced but did not initiate.

Was she maddened by my unquestioning optimism as I brushed away her anxious doubts? Did she too feel guilty as we scrambled through these chaotic days? Impossible to tell.

The two little girls whispered and giggled, heads together and hands busy as they rearranged the doll's house. Nick lay stretched on the floor playing with a long line of buttons and hissing through clenched teeth in the way of small boys; his mind a thousand miles away. Were the buttons soldiers, ships, trains, motorcars, animals? Who could guess as they all engendered the same grinding hissing sound like an ancient car in bottom gear.

Adrian chuntered up and down the passage and with occasional squeals and exclamations, every so often peered round the door, his blue eyes brimming with fun like a rollicking puppy making sure we were all still there.

I cheered up a little; they didn't look like neglected children.

Although Nick and Christel's ears must have continually burned with cries of, 'Hurry now, do be quick. Come along and do get a move on. Please get dressed and don't dawdle. Hurry, hurry.' We were always rushing them, but there was no alternative with so much to do.

Lu and Adrian were in and out of every venture like darting needles. Almost without explanation; knowing what was being planned, hopping from foot to foot they waited expectantly whilst we threatened and cajoled the slow pair, who looking at us vaguely, after hours of prodding and would ask.

'What did you say? What are we going to do?' and be astounded when we told them.

We must on occasions have gone out to look at the sky and smell the countryside, but I cannot remember one single moment when we really stopped working.

Now that the men had actually started in the hotel, we decided to move to Exmouth shortly before Christmas. This would save rent and at the same time we could keep an eye on all that was going on. There was a great deal of furniture, which we wanted to paint ourselves. After disentangling items from the rest, gradually we would furnish each room as the men finished, hang the newly made curtains, stain the floor, tiptoe out locking each door firmly as we finished. In this way we hoped to introduce order into chaos. We thought it safe to say we would open for Easter.

If our own four children were to be accepted by other people we would have to welcome families. So for the past few weeks we had been inserting a weekly advertisement in the Nursery World and The Lady, assuring parents of a warm welcome and extolling the delights of Exmouth. Each evening we attacked the growing pile of letters, laboriously writing by hand. If only we had a typewriter we moaned.

Neither of us could type, but we felt sure we could learn. One wet afternoon when we were all cooped up in my small sitting room; the children breathing heavily through blocked noses and everyone irritated with everyone else, I decided to clear the cupboard under the stairs.

Throwing out a broken horse, an old rug, several deck chairs, a battered Spanish hat, I suddenly let out a yell. Everyone crowded round, as emerging backwards and dirty, but triumphant. I brandished an almost new U.S. Navy typewriter. What a find! However had it got there?

Then I remembered that early in the war I had let the house to a young American and his bride. They had been bad tenants; leaving hidden a large burn hole in the sitting room carpet, which they had carefully covered with an armchair. They had left the district months before I discovered the damage. I scored the loss up as one of the hazards of war. But here was compensation, as it would be impossible to find the couple now and I certainly wasn't going to worry the U.S. Navy over such a trivial matter.

No, this was a miracle, and should be accepted as such. We would now be able to give the illusion of being experienced hoteliers. Once we had mastered the art of typing! There was one small hitch, this typewriter only dealt in capital letters, so all we wrote had an air of dramatic urgency. Also our spelling mistakes stood out rather too obviously. But maybe that too would improve with practice.

CHAPTER 7

THE MOVE TO THE SEASIDE

T he man says he can't take us in the van. He says he can only take the goods. What are the goods and why can't we go?' Nick gazed at me anxiously as two disgruntled men pressed past me in the narrow hall.

'We can't take passengers, we're not a bus;' said the taller of the two tetchily, his face as crooked as the hind legs of a bulldog.

Dismayed but determined to be cheerful, I shushed the children's wails and bundled them into the garden. 'Never mind. You must be good and helpful and we'll have fun in the bus.'

My mind reeled at the thought of a three hour journey with three changes and four crotchety children, but I was determined to remain on good terms with the removal men hoping the children's disconsolate faces would gradually win them over.

It was a sparkling day with fat white clouds racing across a dazzling sky. There was a hint of snow in the air. I bundled the children into thick winter coats, crammed on bright woolly caps and they sprang about like newly released pit ponies scrunching the ice on the puddles whilst keeping a wary eye on the two men.

Gerdy had gone on ahead in the car armed with buckets and brooms and Mrs. Furzle. Mrs. Furzle had helped us intermittently over the past few months and though she had not much idea of cleaning, she had been invaluable. A tireless talker; her greatest virtue lay in her love of children. We could always be sure that when we returned exhausted from a long day in Exmouth we would find the children grubby but cheerful, with Mrs. Furzle ambling amicably in their midst. Her lined pink face was as pleated as the underside of a mushroom. Never irritated, she kept up a steady flow of broad Devonshire. Lu had confided a little doubtfully that 'Mrs. Furzle was a nice lady but I don't like it when Adrian cries, cos she makes us sit on the floor to watch while she takes out her teeth. She pops them in and out to make him laugh'. But on balance, even with this macabre form of entertainment the children were fond of her.

I organized the children to collect scattered toys into two large sacks and then helped our new acquisition, Betty, to strip the beds. We realized some weeks before that if we were going to be free to get any real work done we should have to have regular help. Through an advertisement in the Nursery World, we had been lucky in finding this cheerful Lancashire girl, just de-mobbed from the ATS (Auxiliary Territorial Service). With a mass of bright yellow hair, a pretty face, a startling vocabulary and exceedingly bandy legs, her robust sense of humour and slap happy approach to life made her an ideal companion for the children in our irregular household.

Whilst the men worked stolidly, I made an optimistic mountain of sandwiches, packing them with four large bottles of beer and some milk. I could feel the atmosphere becoming steadily warmer as their small assistants staggered out to the van with anything they were allowed to carry. Over the months they had become adept at avoiding our frenzied scurrying and were therefore of real help.

By noon Alf was saying 'These little uns could come along wiv we, they won't hurt. Bert 'ere ' will just fix up they mattresses at back there and then cum she roll they chillun lull be zafe and zound.'

It was sad shutting the front door for the last time on 'Greystones' the little house which had seen so much carefree happiness, so much anxiety and sorrow. It was here that I had heard of the deaths of so many of my pre-war friends. It was here that Gerry and I had loved and fussed over the babies. Here too that we had said our last goodbye as we listened to the continuous thrum of German bombers droning overhead on their nightly path to the Midlands. It was our roof that housed the town siren and its horrible whine, which had woken Lu nightly all through her first two years. It was from the top window of the little house that I had watched the American troop carriers crowd the sky on their way to invade France.

Was it only twenty months ago that five pregnant young women had arrived in one day, when London's buzz bombs were at their worst? For one ghastly week three new born babies, five sensitive nervous mothers, two over-worked district nurses, myself, Lu and Nick had all struggled for baths, clean nappies, space in the airing cupboard, clothes lines, reassurance and love. The little house had gallantly held us all in its warm embrace and I was sad to leave.

It was a splendid journey. The children enthralled, packed in with all the furniture; Alf and Bert by now quite won over, entered into the spirit of things, changing places every so often so as not to miss any of the fun as we rolled about on mattresses.

We giggled so much that Adrian got hiccups and had to be resuscitated with sips of milk. Then Alf laughed so heartily that he got hiccups and had to be cured with sips of beer. In no time at all we drew up at The Seagull clambering out to exclaim and rejoice over our new home. The bay was at its polished best with wind tossed waves, screaming seagulls, wheeling and circling over the leaping sea. Nature herself seemed to be echoing the children's excitement and joy.

Gerdy and Mrs. Furzle had worked so hard that even with no furniture the basement had a look of home with a big kettle steaming and toys strewn around the sunny front room, which was to be our home. We sat on packing cases eating our picnic whilst Bert and Alf told us of past moves and eccentric clients. Then whilst the men unpacked the van, we slipped out to see the children's first reaction to the shore. Armed with crusts from sandwiches we stood on the beach in the centre of the circling mass of screaming gulls and squealing children. As we watched we knew we had done well in bringing them to this beautiful place; hoping that perhaps the sea with its rich treasures would make up in part for the loss of their fathers. With thankful hearts we turned and leaving Betty to guard them on their first tour of discovery, we entered the hotel to start phase two of this exciting new life.

CHAPTER 8

APRIL 1947 – FEMININE PERSUASION

We heard unofficially that we were called the 'plump one' and the 'thin one' and could never decide which of us inspired the greatest degree of active work from the men. Gerdy had an excellent technique, which could transform the laziest of workers. She would gaze into bemused eyes, cooing in a voice as smooth and silky as egg nog,

'Now zen old man, shall ve do...'

It was amazing to see how rapidly things took off under this treatment. Unfortunately, the moment she took her eyes off the dazed man the chances were his mates reduced his debilitated mind to a jelly with their ribald ragging, he was then useless for the rest of the day. Unless I followed in Gerdy's wake, gently shaking the entranced one back to life, tactfully distracting his joking mates and then with some firm persuasion the work would continue at remarkable speed.

Wasn't it Gauguin, who is reported to have said that, he was tired of painting women with apple shaped 'derrières' and would his friends please find him pear shaped ones. I could see his point, as Gerdy's intriguing pear shape, clad in tight black trousers, backed out of room after room as she completed the gleaming stained floors. If I could appreciate the line and symmetry of her neat behind, our twenty men appreciated it even more! There was never any hint of trade union rights as carpenters, plumbers or plasterers jostled for the painter's job, which would bring them close to Gerdy!

Gerdy, a fanatical worker, threw herself into every job with fierce energy, never leaving things half done however exhausted she felt. It was her example, which inspired us. I for one would have packed in each task far earlier had I not had her lead to follow.

Les, the carpenter, a tall morose but handsome man with black hair and vivid blue eyes, never had much to say, but he sawed and hammered steadily, winning our admiration by his speed and skill. His mate, a thin disgruntled man, grumbled in a low monotone alongside Les, who treated him with lofty indifference.

Patrick, the head painter, the most popular of all was big, blond and easy going. He never hustled his men, yet they achieved a mass of work each day. Gentle with the children, he was always willing to put a lick of paint on old toys.

Charlie, the plasterer, was an artist. He loved his work and even the dullest wall could bring a look of ecstatic pride to his whiskery face. If we allowed him to put a squiggle here and there, his pride knew no bounds. He would burst into a rapturous whistle, which he kept up for the rest of the day. A born comedian, wearing a woolly magenta cap with a green bobble, he slapped and sloshed cement with abandon, while doing complicated things with several buckets and balanced precariously on his ladder. The children adored him, finding the funny man in the pantomime that year a bit of an anticlimax.

Mr. White, the builder, was a splendid fellow. Big, bluff and hearty, he could bellow like a trumpeting elephant and often did; standing on the pavement while directing operations on the roof, with no effort at all. When discussing intimate affairs with Fred the foreman, his whisper could be heard clearly at the end of the road. 'Here comes the whispering baritone,' the men joked as his car drew near.

We had great faith in Mr. White. He had promised us twenty men the moment we got the permit and here they were. He assured us we would open on April 1st and we believed him, but knew it was going to be touch and go.

Luckily he had a deep scorn for ministries and regulations. If he couldn't lay his hands on vital materials and we could, he asked no questions. He just winked noisily, making good use of whatever was produced.

Wood was our greatest problem. The ration allowed £1's worth each month, which was ridiculous. By chance I discovered ship loads of Finnish wood came into the dock every so often. By dint of pleading with and potentially persecuting a chap called Bill who was in charge of these consignments, I managed to persuade him to part with a load every time it arrived. The men were incredibly generous in giving up their monthly dockets and I so confused poor Bill by brandishing these bits of grubby paper under his nose, almost before the ship docked, that he lost his head when it came to doling out planks. Les, his lugubrious mate and I would wait until dusk, then furtively cycle down to the harbour. Muttering at Bill through the side of my mouth (I was quite good at this by now) we loaded the two men's bikes. They wobbled off into the night while I circled around like an agitated sheep dog, ready to cause a diversion should a policeman appear.

It didn't seem to matter to Mr. White whether the planks were the right width or vintage. He was delighted with anything; if too wide or too thick he'd whisk them away and make a deal with another builder for planks of the right size. In this way we managed to get all we needed, but it added another chore to our already busy day as someone had to keep an eye open for Finnish ships sailing into the harbour.

Fred, the foreman, was a silent sensitive chap. In his philosophical way he accepted the fact that Gerdy and I were far keener on getting the work completed than he and that we had our own strange way of achieving this. We suspected that he read poetry in the back yard, whilst we took over his job as foreman.

Tom, the labourer, mysterious, dark skinned and lithe as a panther; his eyes opaque, the same straw colour as his thinning hair, was silently at our side in every crisis. He nurtured a smoldering passion for Gerdy but was tactful enough to appear eager to help me as well. He had been a commando and must have been invaluable in that field. Whatever we needed he had a knack of conjuring from nowhere. He told us this was called 'winning.' Tom must have been the champion of all 'winners'. It was all one to him, a glorious challenge! If as well, he could win a dazzling smile from Gerdy, so much the better.

Our first task at 7.30 each morning was to open the door for the men, bring in the milk and the ever increasing pile of letters, gulp down coffee and then leave Betty to deal with the children's breakfast and housework, then dash upstairs to paint furniture. Most of the chests of drawers and dressing tables we had bought were battered and shabby, but we aimed to make them pretty in colours harmonising with each room.

Our arms ached, our heads ached, we froze, we groaned, we became ingrained with paint and I personally became poisoned, but we gritted our teeth and painted on with our limbs heavy as sodden towels. Our wonderful idea of getting each room ready one by one fell through almost at once, as electrician chased gas man and carpenter got involved with plumber. No sooner had we got one room ready than someone else wanted to tear up floor boards. We could see no clear picture of completion, only chaos. So we stacked our handy work in one big room, praying that no one would scratch or dent it. By lunch time we were so stiff and tired that we could hardly crawl down to the tin bath to clean up, before creeping into the hotel next door for a good nourishing meal.

We did not want to waste time on preparing cooked meals, feeling that if we had one good meal a day, cocoa and beans would suffice for the rest. But like the painting, things worked out otherwise. Our first meal was not a success. We might have known that it couldn't be from the cold hostile reception we got from the Host and Hostess when we originally made the arrangement. He had a long thin sinister face with clouded yellow eyes, which leered at us menacingly. She had cold beady eyes and a mouth as tightly buttoned as gaiters. One look told us that she hated children.

In the glacial dining room we were seated at a table in the centre of the room. Naturally the children giggled, partly from nervousness, but also because they found the frigid stares of the other diners and the tomb-like atmosphere vaguely funny. I felt like weeping. The room seemed to smolder with hate and cooked cabbage. A frosty faced elderly woman sat behind me, making nervous clicking noises with her throat. This the children tried to imitate until pinched under the table into a semblance of good manners. The only other sound was that of scrunching toast, which echoed round the room like soldiers drilling on gravel.

Suddenly a cheerful noise broke into the gritty silence, when canary like twittering floated up the lift shaft. Once again the children dissolved into suppressed giggles. Had the ancient lift finally wheezed to a halt? No, it surfaced with a load of soup. The stodgy waitress slapped down plates. Our host stared at us with octopus eyes, his wife glinting malevolently through her pince-nez. The guests feigned deafness as the twittering lift descended again. A plate of something liquidly evil was dumped in front of each of us. Gerdy took one sip, went pale and firmly put down her spoon. Cad! I thought. That means I've got to eat it, otherwise the children will balk, then Madame will be outraged. I swallowed it somehow. The children plodded on unconcernedly and I thanked heaven for the windswept beach, which gave them such ravenous appetites. Shepherd's pie followed, grisly, grey, dry and unsalted. If this was the nourishing food, which was to keep us going it wasn't a hopeful outlook. With a stern look I compelled Gerdy to eat up so that I could tuck mine under some sea-weedy stuff swimming about on my plate.

Then a mass of tapioca pudding arrived. I loathe tapioca, but it was my turn to eat. Somehow I swallowed the nauseous glutinous mess. Even the hungry youngsters jibbed. Only blonde Betty was seemingly unconcerned, as she cheerfully pushed Adrian's spoon in and out of his protesting mouth, whilst polishing off Nick's share; thus earning his undying devotion. The ATS must have given her an iron stomach. The girls looked at us so pleadingly, we let them leave theirs and we hastily left. Perhaps it would be better tomorrow, but this was doubtful. The place had such a look of stark desolation that one knew instinctively that no good meal had ever been served in that hotel.

'Vell,' said Gerdy, 'There's one good thing about it. If this is to be our nearest competition I don't think ve need worry over much.'

Deciding that we couldn't afford to pay for this horrible fodder out of our tiny income, we agreed to stick to the agreement for one week, as we didn't want to make enemies of our nearest neighbours, but after this we would brew a good Irish stew on the one gas ring. Even if we could only find a few carrots, an onion, an odd bone or two, it would still taste better and be more nourishing than anything that hotel could produce.

'Good,' Gerdy said with resignation. 'But I don't think we need to bother about making enemies. They obviously hate us already. Did you see his eyes?' She shuddered.

About now we decided we had better make contact with the Food Office. As this was to be a vital meeting, we felt it worth taking great care with our appearance in order to woo the head man. We scraped off what paint we could, put on best hats and on elegant high heels tottered off to meet Mr. Kent. I pushed Gerdy ahead while fixing an ingratiating smile on my freshly painted lips as we settled down in his little office.

Gerdy was looking particularly glamorous as she loosened the fur collar of her blue winter coat. With eyes demurely lowered, she gave Mr. Kent a timid smile and then casually crossed legs elegantly sheathed in David's nylons, which we still treasured and shared as occasion demanded.

'Yes, of course the Food Office would be delighted to help in every way.' This was a good start and hope rose. Mr. Kent, a precise man, went on,

'You do realise that you have to keep a strict account of every single person who eats a meal or drinks a cup of tea in your hotel?' Yes, we knew this.

Mr. Kent kept on emphasising how we must make a careful note of how many beverages each person drank. We should have realised from the stress he put on this that it was of deep significance, but stupidly we thought that meat was the important thing, dismissing beverages as a kind of British 'nice cup of tea' joke. We were to learn! However, we felt we had made a good impression on Mr. Kent and if any extra rations were going to be given away we stood as good a chance as anyone, certainly a better chance than those frozen faced neighbours of ours.

Mr. Kent was very taken with Gerdy, which was obvious. She was playing up to him with all the skill she brought to everything she undertook. He once again stressed the importance of accounting for every cup of tea, then showed us how to count and bundle the various tiny squares of coupons. As we left the outer office we were awed to see three harassed women laboriously sorting out thousands of minute squares of paper, tea in one pile, fats in another and so on; right through the ten or twelve rationed foods, which were so scarce. The war might have been over for a year or more, but never had food been so hard to come by. So they really did count each square. We should have to be careful we vowed.

Legal documents were beginning to trickle down from the Midlands and at last it looked as though The Seagull was about to become a proper company. We had to meet our lawyer, Evan, at the Exeter bank the following week. Mr. Gliddon was at the same time going to introduce us to a personal friend of his, whose firm would handle our accounts.

So once again we donned best hats. Appearing nervously at the 'rendezvous' we were confronted by the most fearsome man either of us had ever encountered. He stood, dark and solid, like a lump of Aberdeen granite, looking at us with a sardonic expression. His eyes under tufted brows, hypnotically shrewd, missed nothing. Paralyzed, we crept into our seats. I never took my eyes from his face, knowing exactly how a rabbit feels when cornered by a stoat. Mr. Barclay obviously had little faith in women running a business, however small and paltry. He bombarded us with questions that as far as we could see had no answer.

'How much profit do you expect to make in the first year? How much do you estimate your laundry bill will amount to each week? What proportion of your profits do you intend to plough back into the business each year? Have you worked out the approximate cost of feeding each guest? What budget have you drawn up?'

All we knew was that we should open our doors on April 1st, hoping to fill the place with pleasant people who would want to return each year and with any luck tell all their friends about us. We hadn't a notion what food would cost or how much profit there might be. We just hoped vaguely that with Mr. Kent's help we might find enough food to satisfy everyone and that what we charged would cover the cost of what we provided, with luck leaving a little profit. It would be wonderful if we were able to feed ourselves and the children out of the business.

With prices rising daily and goods shrinking weekly, it seemed to be a waste of time to hazard guesses as to the profit we should make. But to this sardonic man our kind of sloppy reasoning made little impression. He was obviously baffled as to why he had been introduced to this paltry little concern. We could feel him getting more and more sceptical as we fumbled with each of his terse questions.

Evan sat with an inscrutable face. I knew he was hugely amused by this unequal battle, but he allowed us to flounder, stammer, get indignant and then sink into angry silence, before he tactfully intervened.

'Mr. Barclay, I have known my client for a good many years. Her methods aren't always orthodox, nor are they entirely businesslike, but she usually manages to make a success of what she does.'

'So why not leave these ladies to manage The Seagull in their own way and let your firm iron out the difficulties as and when they arise.'

With this Mr. Barclay had to be content. He shrugged, his dark eyes narrowing as he sank into disapproving gloom. We felt sorry for Mr. Gliddon glinting benevolently behind his gold rimmed glasses. He was going to have a tough time with his friend after we left.

'Gerdy,' I asked, 'Why do you think Mr. Gliddon let loose this fearsome man on us?' 'He must have known he would hate everything about our beautiful little Seagull and I thought when he mentioned this friend it would be someone like himself, a quiet chap who would do what we wanted and not bother us with awful questions.'

'I think he did it as a joke,' mused Gerdy. 'I watched him when he was introducing us. He had a most sly expression on his face. Anyway that Mr. Barclay is far too clever for us. He will be extremely disappointed if we don't make £10,000 in the first year. You'll see, he'll be round our necks all the time criticising every single thing we do.'

'Oh Gerdy' I wailed 'You can't mean that, as I know I couldn't do a stroke of work if he was peering at everything with those cynical eyes. Thank heaven he lives in London. He looks so successful, I'm sure he must be kept terribly busy up there. He couldn't possibly keep on popping down here could he?' I was appalled.

'Well Kirstine, don't say I didn't warn you. His mouth shut like a trap when Evan told him to stop plaguing us. If ever a man looked determined to interfere, it was that one,' and Gerdy strode on looking like an outraged Scandinavian goddess.

Daily the bookings were mounting and we could look forward to a full hotel for most of the summer. Several families were due to arrive on the day we opened. We tried to picture what they would be like.

Every afternoon we answered letters, or finished curtains and bedspreads. Then after putting the children to bed, we wrote and sewed some more. We had upholstered the 50 dining room chairs and we almost burst with pride as we stood them in neat rows, their brass studs gleaming on the beech coloured tapestry.

We fell into bed each night in a coma of exhaustion, and then had nightmares about not being ready in time.

The children seemed happy with Betty the blonde bombshell. We were able to keep a long distance check on their movements by observing the men on the roof. Heads turned to the West told us they were approaching from the harbour; heads to the East from the cliffs and all eyes to the North meant the end of a shopping expedition. A chorus of wolf whistles heralded their imminent arrival. This was the signal for us to warm up the Heinz baked beans.

As the days rushed by we began to wonder about staff. We had found a girl, sitting like a sea nymph on our doorstep on a pouring wet afternoon; dark hair hanging in wet streaks over a rain washed wistfully pretty face. She told us the matron from a nearby children's home had sent her. She loved marines, children and housework in that order. Thankful for the marines, who were stationed at Woodbury 2 miles distant, we signed Minnie on as a chamber maid.

The man, who delivered coal, surprisingly suggested that he should come to us as chef. He had been a chef's assistant in the Navy and from the confident way he talked we felt sure there was nothing he did not know about catering for numbers. At that time we were innocently ignorant about chefs, naval or otherwise. His name was Leslie and he was thin, agile and nervously anxious to please.

Later one night he appeared with a chum, who hovered modestly out of sight. Percy, a window cleaner, thought he would like to try his hand at being a waiter. We hadn't thought of anything quite as grand as a waiter. But when we finally caught a glimpse of the handsome shy Percy we signed him on, while admiring all 6 foot of his brawn, muscles and chestnut curls. He assured us he knew about waiting at table. He could borrow a dress suit, so that was settled.

We had always been mystified by Tom, who in his silent way was so efficient. We couldn't understand why he was only a labourer. When we asked Mr. White about this he said cryptically.

'Some men can take responsibility, some can't.' But it was just this gift we thought Tom showed to a marked degree.

We then asked Mr. White if he would mind if we suggested to Tom that he should stay on as our handy man. He gave us a rather peculiar look.

'Not a bit, as I shan't want to keep him on after this job.' He lowered his voice to a throaty roar.

'Perhaps I ought to warn you, he's a funny chap. Nothing special, but he's a lone wolf. The other chaps don't care much for him.' We had noticed this, but felt that perhaps they ignored him because he was only a labourer, We were aware that there were as strict class divisions among the men, as in any other level of society. Mr.Atlee could talk earnestly about equality, but the British public stuck rigidly to their long held prejudices.

As far as we were concerned he could not have been more helpful. Perhaps this too had added to his unpopularity. We knew the men could be jealous and we tried hard not to favour one more than the other. But Tom had been different, always eager and free to help us, so we had accepted him gratefully. Probably this had upset the others. We asked him if he would like the job of handyman and he jumped at it.

Now we had the Ondine like Minnie, gorgeous Percy, Leslie the chef and Tom the handyman. We felt pleased with ourselves; almost like real hoteliers. When in the bank one day, the cashier leaned confidentially over the counter and whispered that his wife would like to help us. She was a trained nurse, but now wanted a change.

She thought that working in a hotel would be interesting and felt she would make a good housekeeper. This was a real stroke of luck. A nurse was bound to be hygienic and we were none too confident of Minnie's capabilities in that direction. Now we could really begin to face the future as April 1st drew near.

The men were working with fierce concentration, but they still had a colossal amount to do. Even Mr. White had begun to look worried when February drifted into March. Every single thing we needed was hard to come by, but it was fortunate that our builders came from good smuggler stock; otherwise we should never have done so well.

We were beginning to get the rooms ready. It was exciting to see each one take shape. One floor was painted in soft primrose yellow another in pale blush pink, with bedspreads and curtains toning in with these two schemes. Each room was different, yet had the same basic colour theme. Now there were four bathrooms, which though small were as attractive as we could make them. The landing, hall and staircase were painted in a soft dove grey and each bedroom door in bright clear contrasting colours. This astounded the men. There had been much head shaking and doubts expressed until in the end they decided they approved.

Charlie, the comedian plasterer, told us confidentially he was going to do the same in his house. His wife was amazed.

Floor boards were laid, electrical wires connected, water gushed through taps, cupboards gained doors, paint brushes worked overtime, but would we be ready in time?

CHAPTER 9

OCTOBER 1947 – ACTUAL GUESTS MEET

NOVICE STAFF

At last the big day arrived. Small groups of painters still lurked in corners. Les hammered in the basement, but all main rooms were ready. Gerdy and I had spent hours dashing from room to room giving a final dust, removing the last of the paint pots, opening or shutting windows, shooing Patrick out as he kept remembering last minute touches. Just before 3.00 pm we stood nervously ready to receive the first guests.

A taxi drew up and out stepped a forbidding looking woman with a small wan husband. Wearing an angry red hat, she stared stonily through our welcoming smiles. Tom draped a varied collection of bags around himself and we trooped upstairs. Their name was Savage and we felt that she at least was well named. Proudly we threw open their bedroom door, standing back modestly to await exclamations of pleasure. We thought the room was beautiful with its primrose walls, soft green bedspread and curtains and wild daffodils in a bowl on the dressing table, but neither Savage made any comment. She directed Tom in stern tones as to where to put their bags, whilst her husband stood meekly by. We felt deflated, hoping the next guests would be more appreciative. We had hardly got downstairs before Mr. Savage appeared looking terrified. His wife had found dirt and wanted to be moved into another room at once. Dirt! Impossible! Everything was gleaming with cleanliness. We had personally brooded over each room with far more attention than our first born infants had ever received. We found the now thoroughly roused Savage standing on a chair glaring into the top of her wardrobe. Reproachfully she held out the red hat, which now had a rim of primrose paint all around the edge. Blast Patrick! He must have remembered the cupboard, crept in when our backs were turned, pushed aside the clean paper and given the shelf a final top coat. Humbly apologising I backed out clutching the offending article to my penitent breast, while vowing silent revenge on Patrick. Though by now we were expert at removing paint stains, Mrs. Savage remained offended until the end of her visit.

The next arrivals were delightful. A handsome youthful Colonel, his ravishing wife, two children of exactly the right age for our little band eagerly watching out for new friends. Within seconds all six were industriously at work in the sand pit. Colonel Vandyke admired everything, remaining undeterred when we found a seagull had flown in leaving its trademark on their dressing table. 'Never mind,' said the tactful Colonel. 'This is bound to bring good fortune.' With these sentiments we hopefully agreed.

Gradually the hotel filled. Exhausted but triumphant, we went to the kitchen to see how Leslie was dealing with his first dinner. He looked cheerful but abstracted, waving us away with cries of 'Don't worry, I'm doing fine.'

We felt faintly alarmed to see our hard sought for chickens sitting on the table propping up a recipe book. For an experienced chef, we felt the dinner so carefully planned should present no problems necessitating cookery books. However, it was best to keep out of his way, leaving him to his own methods, however obscure these might appear to us.

We peeped in on handsome Percy and suggested timidly that cutlery might look better laid straight rather than flung down in the middle of the tables. We tweaked lovingly at the bowls of primroses and lacy table mats, which had taken us months to make. Once again we congratulated each other on our cleverness in buying old walnut and rosewood tables for next to nothing, instead of expensive modern horrors.

The freshly upholstered five shilling chairs glowed against the beech leaf curtains. We felt proud of our dining room. The whole effect was warm and inviting.

'Gerdy,' I said, as we hovered anxiously by the kitchen door. 'I'm not happy about Leslie. We ought to smell roast chickens. Do you think he'd be offended if I offered to help? It's after six and things ought to be far further ahead by now.'

'Vell if you don't I can't think ve shall get any dinner tonight. Vhy not take him a little drink. That ought to give him a boost and couldn't hurt his pride.'

So carefully pouring a good big tot of gin I edged myself round the door. Leslie was no longer cheerful. The look on his face had now changed to one of quiet desperation. He seized the gin, while offering me a choice of at least ten different jobs. We worked like dervishes; whisking from oven to table and from Aga to sink. Dinner was only twenty minutes late. Surreptitiously I flavoured everything, as I was learning my first lesson as to why British hotel food almost always tastes of absolutely nothing. It was a nerve wracking meal with Percy nervously dropping plates, Leslie in a state of near hysteria, Gerdy soothing potential complainers, while wearing a white lacy blouse, long black skirt and dashing red cummerbund;

her air of soignée elegance was impossible to resist. Only Mrs. Savage remained aloof and unforgiving.

We decided that whether Leslie's pride was hurt or not, one of us would have to steer him through all but the simplest meals. Fortunately he realized this himself and was quite pleased if we helped, as long as he was given full credit for every meal produced. His methods horrified us as he dripped cigarette ash over everything, littering the floor with half chewed stubs. When I tentatively suggested that the kitchen was getting a bit messy, he slung down a bucket of water and started to slosh it about with a broom. Remembering the difficulty we had endured in getting the place rewired, I protested vigorously but my remonstrations had little effect. He knew! He had been taught in the Navy how to swill down decks, and this was how it was going to be done in The Seagull. My moans were mere feminine fancies.

Things were little better with Percy, who was work-shy. He loathed laying tables, grumbling incessantly that we didn't have white table cloths so that he could flick off the crumbs as he cleared, as all the best waiters do. Our notion of polishing tables every day appalled him and as for daily hoovering, this was just one more feminine foible. We could see Percy wouldn't last very long.

Upstairs things fared a little better. Mrs. Velta, a severe bossy little woman, as hygienic as we had hoped, kept large bottles of Dettol in every bathroom. The smell after cleaning was overpowering, but we felt the guests must have great confidence in such a show of efficiency. We surmised, but did not investigate too closely, that there was some tension between Minnie and Mrs. Velta. We could sense complaints hovering in the air, but by talking fast and leaving in a hurry we managed to avert any direct confrontation. Minnie drifted about like a wistful mermaid, making a dustpan and brush look like a collection of seashells as she gazed mistily out of windows in the direction of the Marine camp. Mrs. Velta no doubt had a point, but we didn't want to hear it.

Bandy Betty, haphazard, noisy and cheerful, slapped or cuddled the children indiscriminately. Luckily they seemed fond of her, but we were not entirely happy with her methods, feeling a little more of Mrs. Velta's hygiene might not have gone amiss. Whenever we caught sight of them on the beach they were being acrobatically tossed about by marines, no doubt learning the skills of assault courses.

Some of the songs they sang did not sound exactly like nursery rhymes though it was hard to be sure when lisped by toddlers in strong Lancashire accents, for by now they had caught Betty's dialect. But it seemed wise not to interfere. We were learning fast not to peer too conscientiously into absolutely everything.

Tom was invaluable, not only to us, but to guests as well. The house rang with his praises as fathers discovered his art of 'winning'. We caught intriguing glimpses of whole salmon and squat bottles being thrust into the boots of cars as each party left, Tom, with a self satisfied smirk, shaking well greased palms. Instead of tactfully hiding these large tips from the other men, he would crackle notes under their envious eyes. If Percy got 10 shillings we could be sure that Tom would have £1. Of course poor Leslie stuck away in the kitchen got nothing. I suggested to Tom that he ought to be more considerate, but he got so much fun out of teasing, he was loath to give up this pleasure for the sake of peace in the house. We were discovering in ourselves all manner of peculiar female quirks, like wanting the staff to be one big happy family!

We now entered the phase of strange women who drifted in for a few distracted days and just as quickly drifted out. We needed someone to peel potatoes and wash dishes, but this appeared to be beneath everyone's dignity, so it resulted in Gerdy and I coping for most of the time. I found I could peel three buckets of potatoes in thirty five minutes flat. One elegant but rather dirty lady, clad in high heels and a feather boa, took all of four hours.

She wavered around the pantry complaining in a high pitched whine, but soon found hotel work too degrading and left, much to our relief. Then there was Rosie, a buxom woman with wild green eyes and an explosive temper. Everything made her flaming angry. She tossed china around until most of it broke, so she went. The next was a little dwarf who had to stand on an orange box. The children were fascinated and watched her with big eyes as she clambered up and down. We had warned them not to comment on her deformity and they were good about this, but their favourite game became 'being Annie' and helping each other up and down off boxes, saying encouragingly, 'Come along Annie dear, you're quite safe now. Just stretch a little higher. You'll get there.' Annie was willing, but there were so few jobs she could manage that in the end she had to go.

We then tried a very dirty old man, but Sam had an inbuilt objection to clean water, although that was the one thing we did have in abundance. The gigantic boiler, which Tom stoked with zest every three hours, could have serviced a battleship. Sam shuffled round the pantry wheezing and groaning while mixing up a ghastly concoction of greasy water, floating vegetables, bits of bread and cigarette ends. He was furiously offended when we insisted that he start afresh. He only felt comfortable when the water was like Scotch broth. So Sam went.

Even the possible left at a moment's notice and back we were with the dishes and the potatoes. It meant our real work got hopelessly neglected. It was hard to remember what our real work was, but somehow we had to deal with bookings, keep accounts (with the awe inspiring Mr. Barclay in mind) control staff, rearrange bedrooms, listen to guests' endless stories and refrain from shouting at their over exuberant progeny.

Foraging for food was the most time consuming chore. We scoured the countryside for a chicken here, an egg there, until at last we found a sweet old farm woman near Aylesbeare, who was blissfully unaware of wars, rationing and shortages. She promised a regular supply and even the occasional duck.

Fish, which was unrationed, presented no greater problem than waiting patiently by the harbour for the boats to unload, the only hazard being the unexpectedness of what was produced; herrings often, sole sometimes, cod occasionally, rock salmon rarely. Fresh salmon, thanks to Tom, was often on the menu.

On Friday afternoons we drove over to Beer to fetch lobsters as they emerged brightly red and steaming straight out of Mrs. Driver's immense cauldron. Lobsters so tender, sweet and slipping out of their shells like melted butter. At one shilling and sixpence each this was the cheapest yet most delicious meal we provided, yet there were some guests who preferred to play safe with any old fish, as long as there were chips.

Mussels, we gathered at low tide amidst the green webs of weed scattered over the rocks, accompanied by the slopping of wavelets gurgling and sucking on the shingle round our bare feet. Breaking brittle nails, we snapped them from their homes, with the screaming of gulls deafening us as they hovered and circled over the leaping sea. The only snag was de-gritting, a long and tedious business, but so worthwhile when we saw the delight on the faces of the more discerning guests.

On Minnie or Mrs. Velta's day off we worked upstairs and found making forty beds a back-breaking occupation. I soon discovered that by saying clearly and loudly as I walked into the first bedroom, 'How very kind, the So and So's have made their beds. Now that really is sweet of them.' There would be a swift scurry and with any luck those in earshot emulated the So and So's and our work would be halved, but this took careful timing and didn't always work!

One morning the tension between Tom and Percy came to a head, with Percy chasing Tom round the kitchen table while brandishing a carving knife. As far as I could see he had gone raving mad and was determined to carve Tom into pieces. Tom looked scared, having at last realized he had gone too far. I yelled at Leslie, virtuously scrambling dried eggs while stolidly ignoring the whole affair. He grudgingly threw down his spoon, joining me in tugging at Percy's waist, but it was obvious he would have much preferred to have seen Tom dead at our feet. Of course Percy had to go. We were now faced with a full hotel and no waiter.

Then Gerdy had a brainwave. Leslie was becoming more sullen every day. His self satisfied conceit in what we produced was getting on our nerves. She suggested that he might like to become a waiter, whilst we could take turns cooking on alternate weeks. We had by now got over our fears of catering for numbers, being much more worried as to whether we could get at the food before Leslie ruined it. He jumped at the idea. The tips were the real lure, but he said he was finding the heat of the kitchen in the hot weather too exhausting.

As good socialists, we were determined that The Seagull should be run on truly democratic lines. There should be no impenetrable barrier between staff and management. So each Saturday all work came to a halt, whilst we had a conference with everyone putting forward their suggestions. The idea was a good one, of that I am convinced, but perhaps we were not experienced enough to handle it properly or more likely we had the wrong material on which to work. It simply degenerated into the airing of personal grievances.

'Why had Tom pinched Leslie's mop?'

'Why did Betty hang her coat on Minnie's peg?'

'Why did Mrs. Velta not empty the Hoover after using it?'

Everyone it seemed was 'browned off', 'Couldn't care less' and wanted to be quite sure we knew about it.

They sat around arguing over trivialities, whilst we champed with impatience. After a few weeks the idea was allowed to die. In later years if anyone had a suggestion they made it to us privately. We then weighed up the pros and cons, accepted the idea or gave a good reason for not doing so.

Gradually as the weeks went by we gained confidence. We were still over anxious to please and some guests took advantage of this, but on the whole from the visitor's point of view, things were going well.

That first summer's guests were a mixed collection. A very few disliked The Seagull as much as we disliked them. Many had been recently demobbed and were holidaying on gratuities. Some had never had a seaside holiday in their lives, and were as unsure of themselves as they were unsure of what they ought to expect. Those with little experience of travel were hardest to please, but we were learning to control our tempers, never showing irritation however unreasonably people behaved. It was harder for Gerdy, who hated to see strangers fingering her possessions. With my more unpredictable upbringing I found this aspect less aggravating and could greet strangers while feeling they were potential friends.

Gerdy on the contrary felt everyone a possible enemy. Even though she might have grown quite fond of them after a few days, she could never remember this when it was her turn to receive guests. With a look of distaste she would moan, 'Horrible people in No.7. I'm sure we're not going to like them. The children are rude, she is hideous and he looks as though he drinks.' In all probability by midweek she would be telling me how pleasant they were

I felt it most unfair that however much she disliked people; she looked so lovely and smiled so sweetly, that all were enchanted and coming to me to sing her praises. I soon discovered to my chagrin that most people, men particularly, prefer to be disliked by a beautiful woman, than loved by a plain one.

Several guests suggested we should add a 10% service charge. At first we were doubtful about taking such a high-handed step, but when we thought about it we could see many advantages.

Minnie, who was idle but pretty collected big tips, while Mrs. Velta exuding an air of brisk efficiency, being very conscious of her superior position, got nothing. Tom scooped enormous rewards and the lazy Percy had always been well tipped, whilst Leslie sweltering in the kitchen never saw a guest, so he missed out. We knew too, how hard and unrewarding pantry work was and yet no one ever penetrated that way when doling out largess. The 10% would be in our hands and we could make sure that those who worked hardest got the most, so tentatively we added this charge and were quite prepared to take it off again if people complained. To our surprise no one did and in fourteen years only two men said it was against their principles, but as they left nothing it was perhaps parting with their money, which worried them more than their principles.

If only we could get settled with the staff things wouldn't be too bad we told each other, but each week one or other walked out without a sensible explanation. Always some vaguely futile reason, which we knew was never the real one. It was mystifying. It sapped our confidence and meant we were always overworked, bewildered and behind on our chores.

Chapter 10

Beach, Sea and Sand

The children took to hotel life with alacrity, developing cunning in becoming invisible to families they disliked and forming immediate bonds with those they warmed to. We had built an enormous sandpit, which filled almost all the garden. This gave pleasure to countless children. Exasperated parents longing to prise them away to explore Exmouth, tried to persuade, threaten and cajole them with scant success. From dawn to dusk groups of absorbed little people dug, burrowed and exclaimed in high pitched squeals, with more often than not, Nick's voice raised above all others while organising some complex game. Lu and Christel were more cautious and eyed newcomers guardedly before allowing them to join their select group of two.

We had been given an old boat that was upturned and with porthole windows and a door it made a splendid playhouse. We planted easy growing flowers in what remained of the garden, but the battle the poor things endured with sand, wind, drought, balls, babies and snails made it a tough struggle, which only the sturdiest plant managed to survive. Snails were the worst problem; although a veritable Frenchman's paradise, we knew Exmouth's 'bon viveurs' were not so gastronomically sophisticated. However many snails we disposed of it never made much difference. The next morning hundreds more appeared in disgusting clusters on two dilapidated palm trees.

We were nauseated to find that what we imagined to be bark was in reality families of snails clinging tenaciously to one another. We bribed the children to gather them in buckets and on a sullen morning with the sea like an old paisley shawl with flecks of white glinting in its pinky grey silken ripples and its tattered fringe ruffling the shore, we crept to the water's edge. Hoping to be unobserved we hurled them into the sea. The bribe had sweetened the first part of this operation, but the children couldn't bear the final dastardly act and stood in a melancholy row chanting sadly,

'Oh the poor little snails. The poor baby snails.'

So we had to abandon that idea. Instead we had the palm trees pulled out altogether, much to the consternation of Exmouth's older residents who regarded these tattered relics as town property, feeling they lent validity to inaccurate accounts of year long tropical sunshine. In their stead we planted flowering cherry trees in remembrance of the children's 'lost Daddies', while taking photos of the children patting earth around their own particular tree.

If it had not been for the afternoons spent on the beach, we would never have survived that first exhausting summer. The weather was glorious, with week after week of baking heat. If it meant working until midnight and it often did, we felt those few hours were precious, as only in this way could we share a part of our children's lives.

We soon devised a game as a way of combating the strong current, which raced through the sea in front of The Seagull, as the tide ebbed and flowed. Feeling it would be a pity to curtail the children's swimming, we had to make them aware of its dangers. One of us would wade in deep then stringing the four between the other while standing in the shallows.

We sidled out until the starboard mother was almost out of her depth and then holding hands tightly we lay on the current and drifted swiftly downstream. It was like being on a magic carpet. By doing this as a game they soon realized that the tide was strong, but ran parallel with the beach and due to the curve of the bay it brought us into shore, giving us a wonderful free ride of 300 yards or more. It was a delicious feeling gazing up into the dazzling sky or down into the silvery water where strands of green seaweed streamed like freshly combed hair amidst the darting fish.

After landing we splashed our way back through the warm pools, feeling adventurous as we strode past stodgy people who never ventured further than their comfortable deck chairs.

In front of the hotel were steps leading down to the beach and on one side there was a steep wall made ice slippery by the bottoms of generations of children. My uncle, then well into his sixties, spotting this when he came to visit, shouted with glee,

'Why, I used to slide down that wall when I was a nipper, be damned if I don't do it again.'

With that he plopped down, 'swish', arriving at the bottom with a sedate thump. An elegant elderly lady watching with amusement called out,

'I too used to do that when I was a child and what's more I used to do it with you Duncombe.'

They found they were old friends who had not met for forty-five years, so that was the last we saw of uncle on that sunny afternoon.

Of course our four had immediately spotted these possibilities. Down they went on their behinds, on tummies, backwards and then forwards. We could see they would soon have no clothes left. After a few weeks of feeble remonstration we realized something would have to be done; clothing coupons being even scarcer then than during the war.

We found that living in a seaside holiday town was exceedingly expensive.

'Can we have an ice cream? Could we have a donkey ride? May we go on the swings, the roundabout, the little train, the Punch and Judy show, a trip round the bay and on a rowing boat?' rang in our ears endlessly. Like the slippery wall something had to be done, but what?

We then hit on a splendid idea, which worked for many years. We gave each child half a crown (two shillings and sixpence).

'Now listen. Summer is here at last and this is your summer treat. You can spend it as you like, but once it's gone that's the end and no more until next year. When you've done everything and spent it all, you can have six slides down the wall and then no more until next summer.'

The children gazed at their half crowns in awed amazement. Never before had they owned such wealth. In a daze of joy they drifted off stopping at every third step to gloat. And it worked. Solemnly, with deep enjoyment, they did everything and equally solemnly they returned, and had their six slides; counting honestly and not allowing Adrian to cheat.

After this orgy they settled down to the natural rhythm of the beach, grateful for any unexpected treats that came their way, but honourably refraining from pestering us until the following spring, when on the first warm day a wistful voice would ask,

'Is summer here, can we have our treats?'

One of their favourite games on blustery days was to lob a crumpled newspaper into the wind and give chase. Round deck chairs, over sandcastles, through groups of startled picnickers they would hurtle. Occasionally a kind hearted man, eager to do his good deed, leapt to his feet and joined the chase. Then full of virtue would hand the paper to Christel or Lu, who thanking him prettily would let the paper go again. With regret we had to discourage this game, feeling it didn't come under the heading of acceptable beach behaviour, however amusing it was to watch.

Sometimes Bert Hocking, our friend the boatman, rowed us over to the Dawlish Warren. Though well into his eighties he entered into the spirit of our adventures, greatly adding to our pleasure with his stories of 'When I was a l'il lad.'

We loved Bert who must have broken many a maiden's heart in his youth for he was still handsome, lean, bronzed and with an aristocratic nose, plus far sighted salty blue eyes. On the Warren the children could run naked without fear of giving offence, whilst we pottered and searched for cockles and mussels. Avid for new recipes, I asked Bert how he cooked mussels.

'First ee mus scrub all they naasty grit out of ee then ee mus let ee bide and bile but ee mus'n let ee bide and bile too looong me andsome,' he answered seriously. This became a favourite song, which the children crooned as they poked around the rock pools.

'Ee musn let ee bide and bile too loong me andsome.'

We built a fire, boiled a kettle, and feeling like ship wrecked mariners wondered what we would do if Bert failed to return for us. It was here that Nick made his first heroic swim back to Exmouth across the narrow channel at low tide. We stood in a row cheering when he waved from the other shore. After this it became his daily pleasure to swim both ways, but of course all this came much later.

Sometimes swans flew overhead in formation, filling the air with their distinctive wing beat. Everything seemed to move more quickly on the Warren, seagulls, cormorants, sandpipers, waves, clouds and time. Every pool reflecting dazzling light, a newly minted beauty, the wet ridged sand echoing the wonder of it, until we hardly knew whether we were on earth or running in a gigantic mirror world. We returned in the evening tingling with sun and wind, tasting of salt and sunburn and quite drunk with ecstasy at the grandeur of this new world of ours.

It was Bert who taught the children to row when they were older and on misty mornings we could hear his soft Devon brogue floating over the still water,

'In – aat – in, aat – aizy now me lover – you be proper andsome with they oars this maarnin. Lu me lover – in, aat, in, aat, aize your part oar Nick, nar yer starboard oar, me lover, aizy does it.'

If Gerdy and I had troubles, at least we felt the children were carefree and happy. This made up for everything.

Chapter 11

Things Go Bump in the Night

Things went bump in the night from time to time. All four children fell out of their bunks periodically. Nick was an inveterate dawn wanderer. Through a haze of sleep odd thuds could be heard and if, on opening one sticky eye, I saw a faint glimmer of light, I knew dawn was not far off and felt justified in turning over for another short nap. I had given up trying to make him stay in bed, as he never came to any harm; regarding this solitary time as most precious I soothed my conscience with the thought that running around in the cold dawn bare foot and clad only in pyjamas was probably as good a way of keeping colds at bay as rolling Eskimo babies in the snow.

The hotel had only been open a few weeks when I was startled out of a deep sleep by a tremendous crash on my window. Seeing it pitch black outside I knew that if this was Nick then it ought not to be, as it was 2 am. There was another terrific crash on Gerdy's window in the room next to mine and then quick thudding footsteps in the passage, which ran along the outside of the hotel. A third colossal bang was this time on the children's window and I heard Gerdy fumbling for her light.

Shaking with terror I cried out,

'Whatever is it, who can it be at this time of night? They must be mad.'

'Whoever it is must not go round making that horrible noise.

You must do something' said Gerdy severely as she came through the communicating door.

We crept through the hall with fast beating hearts and then peered anxiously at the sleeping children. By now the footsteps had died away and after waiting for several minutes we crawled back to bed; this time with the adjoining door open. We tried to puzzle what it could mean. Who in their right minds would want to dash about crashing on windows in the dead of night? It made no sense; with only one pair of feet, so it wasn't someone being chased. It was clearly ridiculous and yet it wasn't a dream for we both had heard it.

The following night the same thing happened and we were by now thoroughly scared. We got Les, who was still finishing the cupboards, to screw up all the basement windows. We questioned everyone. It was clear someone wanted to frighten us and he was succeeding.

For a few nights there was silence. We began to relax and then it started again, with violent crashes followed by running footsteps. Then a pane of glass in my window was smashed, so we took our story to the police, who were sympathetic but slightly incredulous as the sergeant took down particulars.

'Well ladies, we'll look into the matter.' We felt he regarded us as hysterical females.

'One of my men will patrol your end of the street tonight, but its cats I shouldn't wonder and there are a terrible lot of cats around those parts. They do make a deal of noise with their caterwauling and carryings on.'

He patted us paternally out of the station.

'Fool,' we muttered, 'as if we don't know the sounds that cats make. Cats don't smash windows nor do they leave man-sized footprints in soft earth.' But we were comforted that night to see a dim form silhouetted against the lamp post though we felt the helmet glinting in the moonlight was bound to deter any self- respecting marauder. At least it showed the sergeant hadn't entirely disbelieved our story. That night and for the next few nights, all was quiet.

Then on the fourth morning we were appalled to find the kitchen window wide open and muddy footmarks all over the floor. A small valueless clock had disappeared. The kitchen was on the first floor and the window had a drop of twenty feet below it. Whoever it was had jumped across an eight foot gap from wall to window ledge with the sole purpose of showing us that no obstacle could keep him out if he wanted to get in. It was horrible to think that someone was free to roam all over the hotel.

We might have to get up for one of the children and we stood the chance of running into this madman; for we decided that only a deranged mind would go to all this trouble. It was one thing to think of a maniac running loose outside the hotel, but to picture him prowling about indoors was quite terrifying.

We rang the superintendent and he took this report seriously. He promised to put two men on duty each night until they caught the man. It was arranged that one should be stationed inside by the entrance, so as to have a clear view of the road as well as that side of the house. Tom offered to stay on guard; always ready to make a drama more dramatic he arranged an elaborate system whereby I had one end of a large ball of pale blue string attached to my ankle and the other end tied round his waist. The moment I heard anything I was to pull on my end and Tom would dash to the scene of action.

It gave us confidence to have this ex-commando as well as two policemen taking our fears seriously. The superintendent had questioned us closely as to whether any member of staff might have an over enthusiastic admirer. We felt that hammering on windows was not a very discreet way of handling a clandestine affair, but the possibility had occurred to us. We admitted that on two occasions we had crept into Minnie and Betty's room only to find them both sound asleep in virginal solitude.

In order to have the back of the house covered, I now slept in a first floor room. Twice, just before the crashes I had been dimly conscious of hearing the sound of slipping coal. On this night whilst dozing fitfully I was again aware of the same sound and was wide awake in a second. I pulled hard on the string and to my horror found it was loose. Could it have been cut? Was Tom lying somewhere bound and helpless? Quaking with terror I crept along the passage, which led to the back stairs armed with a slipper. All was dark and silent except for my pounding heart.

I heard a tiny click from the kitchen, then a soft thud from the basement. Which way should I go? Back to the safety of my room or down to defend the children or into the kitchen to face whatever horror awaited there?

As I hesitated, up the stairs dashed Tom looking desperate and out of the kitchen charged the two policemen clutching mugs of tea, with truncheons at the ready. Raising their helmets most politely they hurtled by with Tom in hot pursuit!

But it was a false alarm. I had heard Tom creeping round the yard and the policemen had heard me opening my door. Meanwhile Tom had considerately removed the string whilst making them tea.

On it went, this cat and mouse affair, with Gerdy and me lying night after night alert for sounds, until Nick heralded daybreak. After a short uneasy doze we had to be up working like demons, with our nerves in shreds. We were by now neurotically suspicious. Any man who looked straight at us we suspected and those who looked the other way convinced us. Les spent one night sleeping in Betty's room whilst she joined the children in the nursery, but all he reported was a bat flying against the window.

Gerdy's brother in law came to stay and he poo poo'ed the whole affair, convinced it was all our imagination, but he did promise that if anything happened he would deal with it as he had been with Wingate's army in Burma and he assured us he knew how to cope with night prowlers. Two nights after his arrival I was woken out of a fitful sleep by the soft sound of coal slipping.

Struggling to awake, I heard an unearthly scream coming towards me like an express train emerging from a tunnel. It rose to a demonical shriek, which ended on my pillow. I grabbed the light switch and found Betty hysterical with terror sobbing 'The man, the man, he's in my room.' I wriggled from her grasp, dashed along the passage, but there was not a sound! Why on earth was there no movement from Gerdy and where were the police? Why wasn't Raymond there? That scream had been enough to wake the dead; perhaps everyone was dead! Then Gerdy appeared ashen faced. We pounded upstairs with Betty at our heels wailing, 'Don't leave me. Please don't leave me.'

We burst in on Raymond and dragged him while gasping, 'Come quick that devil is in Betty's room.'

'What, what, who the hell?' he muttered sleepily and then modestly grabbing at the blankets he mumbled. 'I can't come, I'm not wearing pyjamas.'

Swearing, we left the gallant Chindit[1] to his slumbers and dashed downstairs. By now the police were pounding around

---

[1] The Chindits were a British India 'Special Force' that served in Burma and India in 1943 and 1944.

trying to track the source of confusion. In Betty's room we were awed to find large muddy footmarks leading from the carefully wedged open window to her bed.

By now she had recovered sufficiently to tell us she had woken in time to see a man bending down under the dressing table, which fortunately was placed across the window. She bounded out of bed while giving that unearthly scream. As she darted through the door she had even felt her nightdress slip through his grasp.

The police now decided to be super efficient; insisting on searching the whole hotel. At each bedroom door I informed sleepy astonished guests that their rooms were about to be inspected. Drowsily they watched as the two men shone torches in every nook and cranny. One kept murmuring to me in a breathy whisper as he prodded under beds, 'Mam you have made a difference to this place, very tasty I must say. It's wonderful what a lick of paint will do. I used to work here myself in the Palm Court days and what a change.'

But Betty's scream, as well as terrifying us, had scared the villain for he never returned.

A few weeks later I met the superintendent, who looking mysterious and said discreetly. 'I'm afraid I can't tell you all the details, but we've caught that man.'

'We thought your theory of the slipping coal might have something in it so we had our eye on the chef next door. It would be nothing for him to climb on top of the wall and then slither down the coal heap'.

'We went to question him the morning after your girl had that scare, but he was out'. 'When we returned an hour later he'd skipped it and we lost trace of him and then last week the same kind of incident was reported by a woman who lives on the edge of town; crashing windows at 2 am, running footsteps and one night something of little value stolen from her kitchen'.

'Well, we set a trap and copped him a few nights ago and found it was the chap from next door'.

'He'd been a commando and we think he missed all the excitement of jungle warfare, as it no doubt turned his head a bit'.

Anyway, you won't be troubled again.'

Then I remembered the funny bird noises, which had floated up the lift shaft that had so amused the children. I suppose this was the poor chap's attempt to serenade Betty, having caught a glimpse of her golden curls. This had been his sad attempt to follow up the romance, which never blossomed.

We often wondered what the guests made of the night's excitement. Oddly enough no one mentioned the police search and no one appeared to have heard the scream. So perhaps, like Raymond, they put it all down to fantasy.

.

Chapter 12

Staff Problems

We soon found that to run a hotel well required many attributes which we did not as yet possess. It became increasingly evident that one needed the sagacity of a lawyer, the strength of a stevedore, the tenacity of a politician, the humour of a Charlie Chaplin; all discreetly masked by the charm of a courtesan. The talent we had in these directions was as yet insufficient,

The staff continued to be our major problem and things came to a head when Minnie, by now one of our most faithful, told us she was leaving immediately in order to marry a marine. We assumed that he was willing, but later events proved he didn't exist. The young man who had been produced for our inspection was just a casual friend with no intention of marrying anyone, least of all the flighty Minnie. Then Leslie walked out in a fury over some complicated transaction involving a half bottle of ink. Leslie, a champion scavenger made it his practice to dart upstairs as soon as the door closed on departing guests, in order to ransack their rooms. I met him one day with a tray laden with stray buttons, paper bags, rubber bands, old note books, chewed pencils and half finished bottles of medicine.

He explained, 'I like to ave little fings andy. Ye never know they may come in useful.' Feeling this was a harmless hobby I gave him permission to act like a magpie as long as he was absolutely sure that the guests really had left. I didn't want to be confronted by irate gentlemen demanding to have their rubber bands returned. Leslie had found the ink, but Mrs. Velta already had her eye on it, so there were recriminations, accusations and a great turmoil, ending in Leslie marching out never to return.

The following Saturday early in August, with over fifty guests clamouring for attention and all twenty rooms changing, Betty appeared clad in her best acid green dress and announced, 'Ah'm browned auf, ah want to leave now, ah want ma mooney.'

We could hardly believe our ears. Our precious Betty, who had cheerfully seen us through so much and who knew us so well, and our difficulties. 'You can't' I gasped. 'Betty you can't do this, at least give us a week to find someone else, but first tell us what's wrong, what have we done?'

'Ah moost leave,' said Betty with a set face. 'Ah want ma mooney nao.'

'At least give us a few days Betty,' I pleaded. 'You know we can't manage everything and what will happen to the children?' 'They are so fond of you and they will be heart-broken if you walk out like this.'

But she hung her golden head; looking mulish and refusing to give any explanation. We could have murdered her, but we had to pay and let her go. Feeling stunned and resentful we bundled the children into the garden under Nick's absent minded care and while Gerdy tried to cope with my work as well as her own, I rushed round the town trying to find someone to fill the gap, whilst we advertised for a permanent nanny. Mary, the local catholic priest's housekeeper volunteered, as she was free for two weeks whilst he was on holiday.

Red headed, emotional and disorientated, she taught the children to say their prayers, gave them each a rosary and marched them off every day to the Catholic Church. They tolerated Mary for the sake of the rosaries, which they loved and could be seen on the most unsuitable occasions kneeling in a devout row sending incantations to heaven in a strong Donegal brogue.

We then employed an aggravating bustling little woman, a Scottish Norland trained nanny who never stopped bragging about her former employers; all titled.

Nanny, as she liked to be called, despised Mothers and especially working ones who were dashing about and were liable to upset her nursery routine. We could hear her complaining in a high pitched whine, 'Lady such and such neverr came nearr my nurrserries, not like your mithers who are up and doon, in and oot all the day' or 'the Duchess, now therr was a fine pairrson to wurrk for, she neverr interrfered. Every spring we wud go to Harrrods to buy her childrens' sprring ootfits. They didna wear homemade drresses like these' and she'd give the ironing board a vicious thump.

Lu and Christel giggled, ignorantly unimpressed by titles and Harrods, imitating Nursie's rolling rrr's behind her back.

Her last charge, an Honourable, sounded absolutely horrid; never rude and according to Nanny he loved her dearly. We disliked him intensely until he came to tea when he endeared himself by sticking his tongue out at Nanny. Clad like a ploughman, he refused to remove his wellington boots, threw his bread and butter on the floor, upset his milk and behaved as badly as any commoner.

I had noticed Nick becoming withdrawn with me and all was explained when one evening I heard her taunting him 'wha's a wee softie then, kissin and cuddlin his mammie. A great big boy behavin like a wee babee.'

Nick, who wasn't very big at 6½, hated being called a softie. No wonder he'd become evasive, dodging my goodnight kiss. Without regret on either side, we said goodbye to Nanny.

In one of these interim periods I decided to send Lu to a small play school run by the local church held only a few yards away from the hotel. Nick had by now started at Pencarwick School, leaving after breakfast neat and shining in his new brown blazer, returning dirty and dishevelled in time for tea. I reasoned that if I could place Lu in a place of safety for the morning I should feel easier in my mind. So one Monday morning I deposited her at the church hall in the care of a harassed lady with a Joyce Grenfell manner and an agitated hair do.

'Come along little gal,' she warbled gaily, 'Come along, I know you'd like to play with Beryl.'

'No I wouldn't,' said Lu stolidly. Beryl didn't look any too enthusiastic either, so leaving them to sort things out I returned to my desk.

Twenty minutes later I was annoyed to see Lu solemnly digging in the sandpit. I called out sternly 'Louanne what on earth do you think you're doing? You ought not to be here. You should be at the play school with that nice lady.'

'Don't like,' said Lu amiably through her tangled hair. 'Don't like that place, it is dirty.'

'Rubbish' I rejoined. 'It's very nice and that kind lady will be wondering where you've got to, so come along.'

We plodded back to the hall.

But the kind lady wasn't wondering and hadn't even missed Lu. She greeted me merrily with 'Come to take the little gal home have you Mrs. Richards. You're a little early, but she's been very good.' I explained and left Lu surveying the screaming mass of children with distaste. I had to admit she was right, as it was dirty and stifling any uneasiness I returned to my work.

Twenty minutes later there was Lu in the sandpit earnestly digging, this time with her back to the window.

'Louanne you're a very naughty little girl. You must stay at the play school.'

'Don't like,' said Lu, 'Is dirty.'

I was seized with guilt as I looked at her inscrutable face and her firm pink mouth, I could not be certain she was not hiding a wicked little joke behind those smoky gray eyes, but stubborn as my daughter; back we went. Once more the kind lady had failed to notice Lu's absence! By 11.30 I was worn out with trudging to and fro and Lu, though still patiently polite, was equally bored by my stupidity. Any fool could see that it was dirty and that she didn't like it, and was far happier playing by herself in the garden and was no trouble to anyone.

So I gave up the struggle and the subject of play school was never mentioned again.

Gradually we had to face the unpleasant fact that we had a mischief maker in our midst – someone who was unobtrusively sowing discontent among the staff. We pondered over each in turn. Tom, impossible. Mrs. Velta most unlikely. Now that Betty, Minnie, Leslie and Percy had gone there was no one left to suspect, but why had Betty and Minnie and all the others left so abruptly. One night I had a strange dream – a wispy kind of Freudian affair yet all the next day it kept on recurring. I dreamt I was looking at a pile of apples lying in the middle of the sand pit. As I looked the pile began to shift, I bent over to look more closely, a snake began to uncoil. I jumped back in fright, then saw with relief that the serpent was only Tom stirring from sleep. All day I puzzled over this, then tentatively voiced my thoughts.

'I know this will seem a bit like suspecting God Gerdy but could it possibly be Tom making mischief.

I know he's been wonderful, is really the most helpful of the lot, he seems absolutely loyal bu...'

I tailed off miserably.

'Kirstine, no, that is ridiculous' she snapped. 'Whatever can have got into your head? It couldn't possibly be Tom. Vy he is always helping us, thinking of good ideas. He's as keen as we are to make a success of The Seagull. He couldn't vant to see it fail and knows it will if this trouble continues. What on earth made you think of Tom? You know he never mixes with any of the others – he's a lone wolf. No – no – you're right off the rail lines.'

She looked aggrieved, I felt a cad.

'Oh well forget it old thing, it was a silly idea.'

I didn't want to tell her about my dream but I had nothing else to go on.

Then one afternoon returning from the beach for something I'd forgotten I found Tom leaning into the pantry window deep in conversation with a new, rather pleasant woman who had taken on the afternoon teas. Feeling that it was a good thing that Tom at long last liked one of the staff I fetched the forgotten article and returned to the shore.

However, the next morning this new woman having given every indication of liking the job, gave in her notice. Tom shot into my mind. Why the earnest conversation when Gerdy and I were both out of the house. Was it pure coincidence?

The following Friday on my return from the town I passed the garages and through the corner of my eye caught a glimpse of something moving. On going in I found Mrs. Velta nose to nose with Tom. They looked confused, so I called out something friendly and walked on. Now, I thought, if Mrs. Velta gives in her notice I will know its Tom. They disliked each other so intensely, so why should they suddenly be so intimate? The next day Mrs. Velta told me she was leaving, so I begged her to tell me why, but met with a blank stony silence. After some persuasion she muttered something about the work being too much for her and then with a voice choked with suppressed tears she gave in.

'Well, you're planning to get rid of me, so I thought I'd get my word in first.'

'Whatever made you think that?' I gasped, 'You know we've always been pleased with you and told you so on many occasions.'

'If you are so pleased then why have you replaced me? Tom said'. She stopped.

'What did Tom say?' I asked.

'He told me all about the other woman you've found and how she's experienced in hotel work and she's ready now, and waiting for me to go.'

I was aghast. Was Mrs. Velta lying, making mischief about Tom or had he really made up this fantastic story. I thought it best to question them both with Gerdy there. Explaining to Gerdy quickly what had happened, we waited for Tom to arrive.

Mrs. Velta sat rigid, dabbing at her eyes. Gerdy looked cross; a sulky expression on her pretty face and I felt wretched. When he arrived I confronted him with Mrs. Velta's accusation. He looked at me reproachfully, denying everything. How could we suspect him? What had he to gain? This was just a story Mrs. Velta had made up in order to get him into trouble. She had never liked him, which was true, always been jealous of the trust we placed in him. If we didn't believe him, he'd leave at once.

He sounded convincing, but I asked,

'Why then were you talking so intently to her in the garage? If you dislike and mistrust her so much, what could you have needed to talk about so privately?'

'I was imploring her not to leave until the end of the season. I knew you and Mrs. Ramsay couldn't manage without her. I was begging her to stay.'

His dark eyes stared into mine full of hurt and sincerity. Who were we to believe? Gerdy looked even more miserable. I knew which way her sympathy lay; always with Tom who had been such an ally through the heartbreaking struggle of the last few months.

I was nonplussed. What possible motive could he have? What did we really know about Mrs. Velta? She appeared to work well, but how much of that work did she do herself? The flighty Minnie had always maintained to anyone who would listen that Mrs. Velta did precious little and that she did everything.

Mrs. Velta could be irritating, but was she being so right now? Weeping and moaning, 'It's not true, it's not true.' At times she maddened us with her boring stories of hospital efficiency, which to her way of thinking was sadly lacking here.

I was full of misgiving and yet relieved to have cleared up the mystery; for another of Tom's accusations had been that it was Mrs. Velta who had been stirring up all the trouble.

I gave her a week's pay and asked her to leave. After she left the room still protesting, we asked Tom why she should have wanted to make mischief because the fewer staff, the harder she had to work.

He expostulated shortly,

'Can't you see she wants to get control of the whole place? Before long she would have put a wedge between you both. Get one of you out and she would have become indispensible, and then could have done what she liked. She's artful that one.'

He gave a short knowing laugh. It sounded farfetched, yet anything might be possible. I felt uneasy; that silly dream kept running through my mind. Gerdy had the melancholy satisfaction of being right, as she gazed at me with sullen smoky eyes.

A week later I popped back unexpectedly and found Tom in earnest conversation with Mrs. Velta's replacement, a fat lazy woman who was sent by the labour exchange.

As I came into the kitchen where neither of them should have been at that time of day, there was an awkward silence.

I knew at once from the ugly expression in Tom's eyes that he had been making mischief. The entire trusting friendly look had gone and in its place was an evil hard knowing stare.

I asked him to come to the office. He didn't even try to bluff this time. Furious, he picked up a heavy poker and flung it across the kitchen, not quite daring to throw it directly at me. I could see from his flushed face and the murderous look in his eyes; that he longed to kill. So that was the end of Tom.

The war might be over but we civilians had inherited much of the hatred, which had been so carefully trained into these courageous men. It was a sobering thought.

That too was the end of our staff problems. From then on we had the occasional bad patches, but never again were we to grope our way through a morass of mystery and suspicion. From time to time another trouble maker cropped up, but never one as subtle as Tom. Always before too much damage had been done, they gave themselves away and we were able to get rid of them.

Sadly we realised there is no cure for a mischief maker, in all probability they are wholeheartedly on your side like Tom and want all your affection and trust, and in this way they

gain control; The very crime of which he had accused poor
Mrs. Velta made us feel very guilty and we wrote to apologise.
She never answered.

As well as being the end of our staff problems, it was also the
first hint of disagreement between Gerdy and I, for she never
quite forgave me for exposing Tom. Nothing was said, but I
knew she felt the same sense of tremendous relief now that
things had settled, but she had found it comforting to have
his adoring shadow by her side. Now and then she would raise
her hands to her face and give a deep sigh; unconscious and
profoundly touching. I knew she was restless and unhappy in
this strange world we'd created. Beautiful, intelligent and strong
minded, Gerdy hated being thwarted and our relationship now
underwent a subtle change. From leaving me free and even
encouraging me to make most of the decisions, she now began
to question everything. Usually after a few hours of strenuous
argument and a few more of strained politeness, a compromise
was arrived at and our basic fondness for one another re-asserted
itself. I was no doubt irritating as I seethed with new schemes;
each one to Gerdy more anxiety provoking than the last.

The waste space in the basement nagged me. There was
an enormous draughty dark hall, which inevitably collected
rubbish and a lavatory, which could have comfortably housed
a three piece suite, plus a windowless room that was only fit
for the storage of goods we did not possess. With space being
so precious it seemed idiotic not to use it in the best possible
way. I was all for knocking a wall down here, throwing up
an arch there; creating a new dining room and kitchens and
thus giving us three more bedrooms, but Gerdy viewed these
suggestions with horror, so reluctantly I had to abandon any
idea of further alterations. She also found hotel life distasteful

and to make it more tolerable, she filled any spare moments with
a series of pointless love affairs. I was all for this if it kept her
happy, although it meant I had to cope with everything whilst
she embarked on, or wound up, one abortive passion after the
other. Naturally my protests irritated her. I would then feel
guilty for seeming to be a spoil sport and have to change the
subject with my usual half-baked brightness; thus a small cool
breeze fluttered uneasily between us.

Shortly after Tom left Elsie bustled into our lives. Plump,
jolly and bossy Elsie Hocking ruled the bedrooms, the guests,
their children and me, with masterly skill.

The widow of one of the Hocking brothers, she had more
than a hint of gypsy and quite a few Romany ways. Exasperated
by her bossiness, maddened by her untidiness, I still loved her
for her kindness and humour.

I soon gave up inspecting bedrooms, for she took this as
an affront to her dignity. With methods peculiar and bed
making disastrous; she managed by dint of bluff and charm
to evade all criticism from guests for the next thirteen years.
Children adored Elsie; she not only remembered their names
from one year to the next, but that of their dollies and teddies
as well. She was an inveterate chain smoker, maintaining she
only smoked rarely and, of course, never whilst on duty. I was
on tenterhooks whilst talking to her, knowing that if she hadn't
managed to park her cigarette in some dangerous place, like
the airing cupboard, her fingers were probably being burnt to
the bone as she stood with hands hidden, with smoke rising
in blue wisps from behind her curly black hair. In every room
she left a tell-tale smudge of ash. I grew adept at nipping ahead
of new arrivals and whilst they admired the view, I was gently
rubbing the tell-tale marks away with my foot.

The cooking problem was now solved as well. My sister Eileen Rasmussen, alias Cookie and six years my senior, was recently de-mobilised from the A.T.S. and came for a few weeks whilst she made up her mind what to do next. Her visit lasted for seven years.

Cookie was in her own distinctive way a raging eccentric. Nothing could deviate her from her chosen course and some of her courses were exceedingly devious, but she was a magnificent cook. For that we forgave her much.

A great talker and always 'behind', every meal became a small miracle, as nothing was ever started in time. The milkman, the baker and the butcher were all hailed with cries of 'There you are, I've no time to see you now. You're late and I'm all behind, so you'll just have to wait until I have a minute', then feeling conscious stricken for being so brusque and in order to make amends, she would start a long conversation, which might go on for half an hour. The wretched man would stand there heaving his basket from arm to arm, first on one foot and then the other; longing to go but loath to offend and anyway unsure of how many or how much he was meant to leave. At last when he did tear himself away, she would cry 'There now, that wretched man, how he has kept me talking. They say women talk but my goodness these men!'

'Now, you'll all have to help, I'm all behind, so just chop up those carrots, stir that pudding, beat up those eggs, count the plates. No. Not that way silly. Now where have I put my knife? Drat that child! Nick has run of with it again. Nick, Nick, where are you? Oh there you are and you haven't got it! Well, where can it be?' Off she'd go chuntering and muttering until the next interruption. Everyone loved her, but also felt sorry for her, as she managed to look on the last lap of exhaustion even on her best days. Being a bad organiser but a loving cook, she never took time off and so would get more and more irritable as the day wore on. After serving dinner, when she might have eased off, she would start a furious campaign of scrubbing the kitchen floor or washing hundreds of dusters, not because it was her job to do this, but I felt in order to make me feel guilty and everyone else indignant on her behalf.

All through the night one could hear scrubbings, bangings, and shufflings as her poor tired feet slip-slopped around the kitchen. This of course wrung the hearts of the late night guests who, peering in at my distraught sister, with turban awry and hair disheveled, felt that this was slavery at its very worst. It was no use saying the next day when they asked in pained voices

'Is it really necessary for Cookie to work so hard? Couldn't you provide her with some help?' I said that she did this because she liked it and they just looked disbelieving, and went away convinced that I exploited her for my own evil ends.

But she could and did do miraculous things with food. All this time we were fighting a losing battle with the Food Office, but Cookie produced remarkable meals from a few herbs, a scrap or two of gristly meat and a tremendous amount of love. She crooned into her pots, whispering amorously at the bubbling brews and patting the Aga, while stirring with a passion all manner of weird concoctions. She really enjoyed the challenge of producing appetising meals for fifty out of next to nothing and was willing to experiment with any kind of ingredient. Somehow from out of a kitchen seething in muddle and invective, delicious meals emerged.

Cookie too was another heavy smoker and she held long involved conversations with a cigarette dangling from her lips. No amount of pleading deterred her, because she was convinced, like Elsie that she smoked rarely and never ever whilst on duty.

'But Cookie you've got a cigarette in your mouth now' I would scream, only to be met with a haughty, 'I never smoke whilst I'm cooking. It wasn't allowed in the army, so I'd certainly not do it here!'

A silent war raged between Elsie and Cookie, each guarding their rights with jealous tenacity. Elsie was responsible for the afternoon teas; usually making her sandwiches before lunch and as milk, butter and eggs were always in short supply it necessitated underground warfare, with Elsie nicking these items every time Cookie's back was turned. Aware of the danger but unable to keep her eye on Elsie all the time, my sister grew more baffled and suspicious. Both were far too dignified to resort to point blank warfare, as Elsie's vast waist became yet vaster as she stowed away her loot.

Shortly after Cookie arrived we had another stroke of luck when Brenda appeared. Pretty, lively and intelligent, with curly dark hair, lively blue eyes and a trim figure that was well rounded in all the right places; she wore her clothes with an air of confidence that was most appealing. Having lost her parents as a child she adopted us as her family, slipping into our lives as though she'd been with us forever. At 20 she had unusual authority and poise. Having decided she wanted a less hectic life than that of a staff nurse in a L.C.C. nursery, she was delighted to find a job by the sea after so many years in bomb stricken London. We all loved her and she stayed for the next five years until her marriage, which was held at The Seagull. The children could not have been more fortunate in having such a delightful companion, as she introduced a balanced regime of songs, stories, cuddles and laughter.

However busy we were, however much we had to neglect them, we knew they would feel little loss with Brenda in charge.

Since Tom left we had been trying to find a reliable handyman, but this was not easy. One splendid fellow arrived; he had served out East and was a most superior type, but we offended him deeply by asking him to keep the dustbins clean. It seemed that not even a coolie would do such a menial task, so out he marched. Once more Gerdy and I were left with the 'less than coolie' jobs.

Then an ancient man, smelling horrible and who was deaf and indignant; presented himself. We had to take him on as there was no one else, but he wheezed and groaned so much that most guests carried up their heavy luggage; leaving him to bring the odd book or pair of shoes. He managed to make even this seem like gross exploitation. He had worked for a local doctor and when I rang to ask whether it was all right to employ Mr. Bouncer as he seemed so fragile and wheezy, the doctor's reply split the line.

'Mrs. Richards,' he roared 'if you can get any work at all out of that old phony, you will deserve a medal.'

In a few days we realised that it was simpler to look after the boiler ourselves and let the guests continue to carry up their own bags.

At last a young man appeared, handsome, energetic and full of fun. Frank had six younger brothers who were all so devoted to him that they willingly did his work. We soon grew used to meeting a long Indian file of men and boys with Mumpy, their Aberdeen terrier that was like a demented outrider, bringing up the rear. All except Mumpy carried buckets and coal hods, all wore gaily coloured caps. From past arithmetic lessons, I felt that seven pairs of hands doing the work of one should have accomplished any job in one seventh of the time, but it didn't work out like that. All had to be greeted and admonished by

Cookie, 'Ah, here you are boys, late as usual. Now you there, take that bucket, move that pan and don't drop that ash. I want you to move that cupboard, catch that mouse and mind you all wipe your feet. Men, men, why are they all so helpless? Not that way silly. Now boys, stop fooling as I'm all behind this morning.'

The cups of tea had to be passed round and all of us embraced in turn as we appeared, while local news was brought up to date. Possibly a little proselytizing took place as Frank and his brothers were earnest Jehovah's witnesses, but all was merriment and warm good humour, rather like Christmas every day. We liked Frank and wanted to keep him, so Gerdy and I revised our normal procedure of saying clearly what we wanted done. We had noticed the other men reacted badly to this straight forward approach and from now on we decided orders should be given and criticism made in writing. It worked like magic.

We found we could write anything; however acrimonious and it was received in silence but acted on; masculine pride was assuaged. Frank and his brothers remained erratically as 'handyman' for the next thirteen years.

Though still far from attaining the perfection necessary to be good hoteliers, we felt we were in our stumbling way making progress. Now at last we could turn our full attention to the guests.

CHAPTER 13

THE PLIGHT OF WINTER RESIDENTS

Winter residents differed greatly from summer visitors and with luck and careful planning they rarely overlapped. If they did, there was certain trouble as jolly families seldom recognised the importance of Mrs. Belcher's special chair and Colonel Trumpet's pet dislikes. My life became haunted by gentle conversations beginning 'I think you ought to know.'

Winter residents were on the whole sad people who had, for one reason or another, given up their homes and were wandering like Bedouins from one hotel to the next always hoping for but never finding perfect pasture land. By and large they didn't like children, they hated young folk who left doors open and most of all they disliked people who upstaged their nostalgic reminiscing.

Mrs. Suffer, a mincing pretentious woman with a spying false friendly manner, masking an obsession about noise, diet and the other guests, returned to us every autumn and left us reproachfully just before Easter. She never could accept the fact that we were a holiday hotel, primarily geared to welcoming families, so from Christmas onwards her complaints lessened. By March she was imploring me to allow her to stay on through the summer.

'But Mrs. Suffer,' I would say patiently, 'You know we arranged all this last October and you took your room at greatly reduced rates on the understanding that you vacated it at the end of March. It is now booked solid from Easter right through until late September. It is impossible for me to let you stay on and even if I could you know you would hate it with children thumping around all day long.'

'But I didn't think you'd turn me out like this. Where can I go? Where can I turn?' She would roll anxious eyes at me dramatically. 'I know you will help dear Mrs. Richards. You are so kind and my only friend.' She pressed my unwilling hand in hers. 'Surely you can rearrange the rooms just a little bit, you have so much space.'

Her arms waved in a wide sweep. 'I love little children, why everyone says I was made to be a mother if...' her voice broke and the faded childish eyes filled with tears. 'If I hadn't lost my dear one. We widows must help each other and stick together.' She clutched my hand again while looking earnestly into my eyes.

'Innocent little children are my only consolation these days so please Mrs. Richards find me a corner, anything will do.' This from a woman who complained bitterly if a baby dropped a teaspoon on the carpeted dining room floor and who insisted on a double bedroom overlooking the sea and three hot water bottles on cold nights.

Mrs. Suffer found life insupportable and manoeuvred guests and staff into supporting it for her. In some subterranean manner she had managed to sign on with at least six doctors who, in ignorance of each other, prescribed wicked looking pills of variegated hues. Periodically she got muddled, took too many and was carried out in a comatose condition, much to the macabre pleasure of the Chess Club members who met twice a week at The Seagull and watched with prurient glee the prostrate Mrs. Suffer stretcher borne to the ambulance. After a few days in hospital she convalesced for several weeks in a nearby nursing home, paying thirty guineas a week and then returned to The Seagull to complain at having to pay six guineas a week.

The end of Mrs. Suffer came abruptly. Her attentive doctor, an earnest trusting woman, decided for some obscure reason to make Cookie chief pill administrator, probably because she was up and about most of the night.

'Now Cookie,' I heard her say. 'Mrs. Suffer is to have two blue, one maroon, one green tablet last thing at night with a little warm milk. Only if she can't sleep and is quite desperate you can then give her two yellow tablets.

Cookie was the last person who should have been entrusted with such a delicate assignment. In the first place she hadn't a very good memory; secondly she felt Mrs. Suffer should pull herself together. (Cookie having been brought up by my mother believed that life was hard and full of effort.) Thirdly, at 2.00 a.m. her feet ached and she'd had enough of guests.

Down would come Mrs. Suffer to plead for more pills and Cookie would grudgingly ladle out three or four, not greatly caring whether they were yellow, purple or green, then pack her back to bed. One morning Elsie unsuspecting, presented Mrs. Suffer with her customary breakfast tray and was appalled when the slumbering lady sat bolt upright, and throwing both arms in the air she shot the tray and all its contents straight up to the ceiling! She then fell back with a thud, whilst cornflakes, eggs and bacon settled tastefully on her lifeless form. Her faithful doctor arrived and a few minutes later stormed into the kitchen where Cookie was frenziedly stirring porridge.

'How could you Cookie, how could you be so stupid,' thundered the doctor. 'You've given Mrs. Suffer an overdose of sleeping pills. You might have killed her.'

'Here, steady on,' said I, who could grumble incessantly at my sister, but resented others having a go. 'Cookie should never have been in charge of those ridiculous pills, but just you come upstairs,' and I marched her back to Mrs. Suffer's room. Dramatically I flung open the wardrobe, the bedside table and the chest of drawers; all stuffed with cartons and bottles prescribed by Mrs. Suffer's platoon of doctors.

Much shaken, the good doctor attended to her patient and we heard no more about Cookie's misdemeanor. But we still hadn't finished with Mrs. Suffer. Not only did she have several doctors, but we also discovered that she had several psychiatrists who one by one came to implore me to keep her on as a permanent guest. Her relatives had now decided they would pay any sum I cared to ask, if only I would relieve them of their burden.

I was assured The Seagull was the only hotel that had taken the good lady back after her first visit, she had been happier with us than anyone. I wondered a little cynically why no one had thought to tell me this before and perhaps offer a more realistic weekly fee. But by now we had all had more than enough of Mrs. Suffer and her pills, so without regret I passed her on to the luxurious nursing home.

Another winter guest was Mr. Ponting. He was very old, rather deaf and wandered in absent mindedly from nowhere with a large trunk. Every Monday morning he trotted off to the town and every Saturday he paid his bill by cheque. Apart from these two activities he sat by the window watching seagulls. After several weeks of this Elsie came to me looking anxious.

'Boss, I'm worried about Mr. Ponting,' 'His room is full of pound notes and when I make his bed they fall out of the sheets. When I fold his pyjamas they drop out of the sleeves. Now he's stuffing them up the taps and I don't know what to do.'

Sure enough, pound notes fell out of every nook and cranny. In just a few minutes I collected ninety pounds and so down I went to have a word with Mr. Ponting, but he was an elusive old man and hated to be cornered. 'It's not safe,' I yelled, 'It's not safe to have all that money lying around.' 'Yes, lovely day;' he agreed amicably.

Eventually I got through to him. Smiling complacently he shouted back. 'But I always cash twenty pounds every week dear lady. One never knows when one will need the odd pound or two.'

'But Mr. Ponting,' I screamed, mercifully all the other guests were out except for one small boy, stolidly watching us with beady eyes. 'It isn't safe and you always pay me by cheque. You never go out anywhere so you don't need all that cash.'

'Yes, my dear. You're quite right, it may come in handy. I like to have a pound or two by me, so I always cash twenty pounds every week just to be on the safe side.'

His kind rheumy old eyes gazed into mine trustfully.

'Have you any relatives?' I demanded, but that led us nowhere, so grabbing his pocket book I found a solicitor's letter and wrote to tell him of my anxiety. His reply was guarded. 'We know our client is a trifle eccentric, but there is little we can do.' etc. etc. So when the time came for Mr. Ponting to leave I found a kindly retired nurse who agreed to look after him. After informing his solicitor I delivered Mr. Ponting to his new abode; he died a few months later festooned in pound notes, after happily cashing twenty pounds every Monday morning.

Two ancient spinsters were with us for one winter. They had never been parted in all their eighty odd years. They were alarmingly undecided; talking in conspiratorial whispers and consulting one another anxiously as to what they should wear, where they should go, and what they should eat.

After lengthy discussions the elder sister would timidly ask for extra hot water, a jug of milk or a window to be closed or opened, the other echoing her bolder sister's request in a deferential murmur. They were in a permanent state of fluster over lost handbags, wrong shoes and forgotten library books. In the middle of a freezing January night I woke to hear anguished cries of 'Violet, Violet, where are you Violet?' followed by an agonised but ladylike shriek and then several muffled thumps. Jumping out of bed I switched on the passage light and was dismayed to see a crumpled Daisy lying at the foot of the stairs.

As I hurtled down the old lady rose, looked around in a dazed manner, re-arranged her nightgown and was off again on her agitated search for Violet. With visions of Violet coasting along the sea-shore with me in chilly pursuit, I caught up with Daisy and persuaded her to sit down whilst I examined her for broken bones.

'No, no,' she cried, 'We mustn't stop. I must find Violet.' Off she went down the passage with me tailing her like a police escort, but no Violet could be found. Eventually I managed to get Daisy back to her room where we found Violet tucked up comfortably and peacefully asleep. Daisy accepted this with no surprise. Having found her beloved Violet she cuddled down in bed, the fright and bumps forgotten. The next morning when our doctor examined Daisy from head to toe both looked astounded, but neither asked who he was nor why he was there, no doubt accepting this as one of life's inexplicable mysteries.

Some of our winter residents were delightful. Mrs. Webb was a darling. Well over eighty, she had a delicious sense of fun and a loving heart. When showing new arrivals into the sitting room we knew that if Mrs. Webb was there they would be greeted with, 'Ah, now, who have you brought us?' 'How nice to see a new face. Come along my dear, come near the fire and tell us where you've come from,' and within minutes the shy newcomer would be happily chatting and feeling truly welcome.

Mrs. Webb had a philosophical outlook and a deep faith. One day she said quite simply, 'I won't live a great deal longer.' A few days later she was poorly and stayed in bed. I offered to get the doctor, but she said, 'No, my dear. I know what's wrong with me and I don't need any help. As long as I can hear young voices around that's all I want.'

A day or so later I moved her down to a room on the ground floor so that we could keep an eye on her more easily. That day she was quiet, asking us to leave her door ajar, but greeting us all with her customary warmth. I took her some hot milk that night and on the way back from my bath peeped in and saw she was asleep. The next morning she was dead, lying peacefully in the same position I had left her the night before. She had died as she had lived and as she hoped to die, giving no trouble and with lively young people around who loved and cared.

Another remarkable woman stayed with us for a few weeks every autumn. I noticed her limping and asked about this. 'Ah,' she said, 'That's quite a story. It's the return of a very old trouble.' 'Do tell me,' I asked, as I followed her into her room.

'Over fifty years ago when I was thirty, I had a bad knee and went to my doctor who sent me to a Harley Street specialist. He diagnosed cancer. After some pressing he told me I had just about six months to live. I was stunned and as I went home I saw a poster announcing the forthcoming visit of a well known faith healer. I had never believed in such things, but feeling I'd nothing to lose I arranged to see this man. We talked, he laid his hand lightly on my knee and that was all. Nothing more, but the knee healed. I showed it to my doctor and he was as mystified as I. He sent me back to the specialist who was equally puzzled, because all signs of the trouble had disappeared.

A few weeks later I was at a party and a woman sitting across the room asked to be introduced to me. She said, without preamble, 'I need you, I am a great niece of Elizabeth Fry and I need you to help me with my work in women's prisons. Will you come?' Of course I said I would and I have visited prisons ever since, teaching the women to knit, sew or read and trying to help them so that when they leave they can lead more useful lives. Now I am over eighty and I know I can do this work no longer. I'm not needed any more, so of course my old trouble returns'. Within six months she was dead.

The fascinating thing about running a hotel is the variety it offers. Maddening people jostle with marvellous people; boring with interesting; generous with mean and sophisticated with naive. Gradually, very gradually, one begins to gain some insight.

PLATES

Kirstine in the 1930's in Honiton at the 'Highland Fling'

Christel, Nick, Louanne & Adrian

Gerdy Ramsay with Christel & Adrian

Adrian & Nick

Brenda – Children's Nanny

The Children's Favourite Pastime - Playing in the Sandpit

The Seagull Team including Rita, Brenda, Cookie, Elsie
Hocking, Gerdy, Kazimir the waiter and Kirstine Richards

Tom - the handy man from Topsham

Kirstine Entertaining Guests

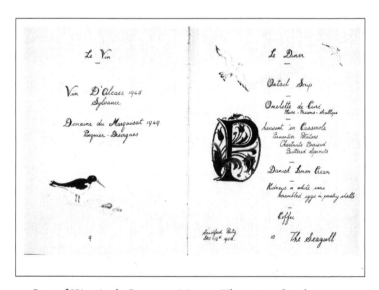

One of Kirstine's Gourmet Menus. The artwork is her own

CHAPTER 14

MY MADDENING MOTHER

My mother's occasional visits did not help towards the
tactful handling of winter guests. She arrived more
often than not in a coach, being the sort of person who could
induce coach drivers to go miles off their scheduled course
in order to put her down exactly where she wanted to be.

With misgiving I would watch a row of jolly faces peering
out of a coach marked Birmingham or Cardiff, whilst mother
waved cheery farewells from our front steps, receiving a
hail of merry salutations. 'Have a good time me dear.' 'See
you next year old friend.' 'Cheerio my love.' Mother had
arrived with nightie in shopping basket and toothbrush in
her handbag.

Having lived frugally for most of her life she regarded the
simplest of hotel living as wild extravagance, maddening us
by announcing to a sitting room full of contented guests. 'I
expect you're all paying far too much. You know there's no
need for my daughter to run a hotel, she has a pension and
needn't work. It's all for effect.' So of course everyone who
had up till then felt they were getting good value viewed
their weekly account with deepest suspicion.

To explain my mother's peculiarities is impossible. I only know that living with her had been most uncomfortable. No fire had ever been lit in any of the bedrooms, any form of indulgence being to my mother synonymous with music halls, night clubs and drunken men at Hogmanay. One was either shuddering with cold whilst rapidly undressing or pressing a rapidly cooling hot water bottle to the most chilly areas of one's anatomy. Even my mother's fox fur had become petrified with the cold while staring reproachfully from the top of her wardrobe.

Mother's notions about baths were that a) they were basically unnecessary and b) if insisted upon should serve a double purpose. This meant that before I had settled in the bath she would swoop with all the dirty linen she could collect. Sheets, towels, pillow slips, napkins, mats and underwear were thrust through the half open door with instructions to leave the water in the bath and give everything a good soak.

In wet seasons this lumber could remain soaking for several weeks and it became progressively more difficult to make the small ration of water allowed have any effect on the slithery cold mush floating beneath one's protesting behind. There was no inducement in any of this to encourage idling about upstairs.

She had her own quite distinctive ideas about cooking. She was a good, if erratic cook. One good blow out, that was that for the week. She was devoted to porridge but had strong ideas as to where one should buy oats. Not for her the wishy washy brands sold in the South of England, so no packet oats ever entered our house. Postcards flashed at irregular intervals to an obscure little grocer in Dundee and lumpy parcels would arrive from time to time, exuding tough leathery smells and trickles of sturdy oats.

Porridge was our usual evening meal, thick, pungent and surprisingly good when eaten with a knob of butter and plenty of salt. Other meals in between this occasional gastronomic feast were kippers or boiled eggs.

Mother fought an endless vendetta with our ancient geyser. This machine was supposed to give sufficient hot water for a reasonably sized bath at three hour intervals, but this was rarely achieved. In the first place the geyser had to be lit three hours before the appointed time and this she could never bring herself to do. To her the fearful roar of the gas jet meant waste, so the time was cut to roughly twenty minutes. Secondly, the geyser lit with a tremendous explosion, rattling the windows and singeing our eyebrows. Thirdly, the geyser's many failures put her in such a passion of rage that she would rush complaining to the builder who had installed it. He soon discovered the little chance she gave the thing, so every encounter ended in loss of face for mother. Can one wonder that she preferred to wash dirty dishes in whatever came to hand and what came to hand was usually vegetable or boiled egg water.

The difficulty of course was that while the water remained hot while we were eating, but by the time the dishes were ready for washing the water had become cold. With this method our dishes were seldom really clean and had to be surreptitiously wiped on napkins before every meal, thus making the occasional bath even more congested.

She had difficult ideas on tea making, insisting on filling the kettle with potatoes or eggs; feeling that both of these would come in handy for a later meal. The resultant tea was very strange, with bits of potato skin floating despairingly among the tea leaves. The potatoes tasted odd too.

Mother had the reputation for being a genius in the art of building fires. I suppose in a way this was correct, if by genius we mean creating scientifically something out of nothing. She would spend much of her spare time rolling newspapers into long wavery sticks and then twisting them into tight knots. These coils took the place of sticks. She would then dampen sheets of newspaper and coat them with coal dust, and then each sticky blackened knob was rolled into an untidy kind of tennis ball.

These took the place of coal. Any other spare moment she spent making paper spills. First she laid the coiled sticks in the grate interspersed with dried orange peel being a great believer in the ignite ability of orange peel. Then a layer of blackened balls were placed one beside the other. On top of this she laid an uncorked-bottle, uncorked because on the few occasions she had forgotten to remove the cork and we had complaining letters from the neighbours and a visit from the police. On top of the bottle was placed another layer of coal dust balls and then a few judiciously balanced knobs of real coal. The whole was then topped up with a solid layer of coke. In the hearth stood a jam jar half filled with paraffin and in this stood a sinister wire affair, which was thrust under the whole edifice at the moment of lighting. After the first fierce explosion the whole thing smoldered sullenly for several hours. An occasional glimpse of orange peel gave one an illusion of warmth and around tea time the bottle began to glow sourly. At about nine o'clock the room began to feel faintly warm and had one been able to sit up until ten or eleven, we would have enjoyed a good blaze, but at 9.00 p.m. sharp mother would peer at me through the gloom saying,

'You look peaky my dear, an early night would do you good.'
So our evening was at an end. The fire was often fiercely alight
in the morning, which made clearing it an unnerving job.

She also had definite ideas about electricity. 'It's bad for
the eyes and it's not at all restful.' So no bulb in our house
was ever of higher wattage than 25. Overhead lights were not
encouraged, so I sat crouched beside a 25 watt lamp, which
mother had placed on the floor behind an armchair, so that
no harm could possibly reach our eyes.

She liked the wireless, particularly religious broadcasts, but
she also liked to stand the wireless in a corner of the hall. This
meant that in order to hear anything the door had to be kept
ajar, so she wrapped herself in a warm Scottish plaid and lay on
the sofa with her eyes tightly shut against the light and kept up
a steady running commentary on the programme. The loftier
the theology, the better she liked it.

'Quite right, quite right, very true, just what I always say,'
she would ejaculate.

So one never heard much of the actual programme and I grew
up permanently cold, with bad eyesight and distaste for religion.

My one ambition was to get married and leave home for
ever, but my mother made courting difficult. For one thing
she did not like young men unless they were making spills,
cutting the lawn or rolling wet paper in coal dust. She also
liked young men to go home at 9.00 p.m. sharp and for me to
go to bed. If we had the courage to sit tight whilst she shifted
furniture, pulled back curtains, switched off lights and silenced
the wireless before she stumped upstairs, it took more than a
normally ardent young man to withstand the barrage of rat tat
tats on her bedroom floor and her wails of 'It's late now, you
must go home, come to bed my dear and go home go home.'

Even as early as quarter past nine, he would be assailed by guilt and slink off into the night, convinced that it must be 3.00a.m. I never quite knew if my mother feared for my virginity or dreaded that we might poke the fire into a good roaring blaze.

But these eccentricities were to help me when running The Seagull. Nothing that even the most bizarre guest did could take me by surprise. I had been schooled by an expert and could regard myself as a professional in the idiosyncrasies of human behaviour, but I considered the mixture was a little too rich when certain guests and mother came face to face.

Chapter 15

Spring 1950 – Things Fall Apart

Three years rolled by. I knew Gerdy had been feeling restless for some time, but I had not realised how bad this had become. In the Spring as bookings poured in, my time was spent juggling with rooms, cots and families. Gerdy had spent most of that winter in the Waldorf cocktail lounge as a student, learning about drinks as we were planning to apply for a table license. When she returned she was in a state of moodiness one day, alternating with a sudden burst of wild elation the next. I took little notice as, apart from all the bookings, new staff had to be interviewed, appointed and then introduced to the work and routine. The children's clothes needed overhauling, the garden needed planting and guests kept arriving. Gerdy's unpredictability was just another 'thing' that had to be surmounted. However, when present she could be relied upon to work hard, either in grim silence or singing hits from 'Oklahoma' or 'Annie Get Your Gun'. On good days her skin shone with glowing luminosity, her lucid green eyes were enormous and excited. Sophisticated and svelte, she reminded everyone of the young Marlene Dietrich, with long slender legs, a voice husky and breathless with its ever so slightly broken accent. She must have added greatly to the Waldorf's attractions.

It came as a shock when she calmly announced she was leaving. At first I thought she wanted to return to the Waldorf.

I choked back a quick protest, then realised she meant she was leaving for ever.

'What do you mean,' I gasped. 'Where are you going? What will you do?'

'I'm going to Australia to join Peter'. She looked at me challengingly.

'Peter. Who's Peter?' I asked.

Then it all poured out. She had met a wonderful man in London and they had at once fallen deeply in love. After a few days of interrupted meetings he had decided they had to be together all the time, so packing her bags she had joined him on a tour of the North of England, where he was buying agricultural machinery for the Australian government.

'Oh Kirstine, he's vonderful. I vish you could meet him. He's everything a man should be; handsome, virile, intelligent and humorous. He vants me to join him in Australia as soon as he has made some arrangements.'

There was uncertainty in her eyes, which she swiftly masked!

'What kind of arrangements?' I asked suspiciously. There was something about her manner that made me uneasy.

She hesitated, eyeing me nervously.

'Vell he's married you see. He vants to get back and fix things with his vife.'

'Gerdy,' I exploded. 'You aren't going to bust up a marriage? How old is he? Has he any children?' I felt shocked. After all she had only known him for a few weeks. It all sounded thoroughly irresponsible.

'He has two boys, but they are nearly grown up. They are ten and twelve. He and his wife haven't got on for years. In fact Peter says they have had no real contact in all their married life.'

I wondered how the two boys could be explained.

'But Gerdy you can't let him break up his marriage. The two children are just at an age when they need their father most. It's nonsense to say they're nearly grown up. What about his wife? All men say their wives don't understand them when they start a new affair. She's probably absolutely devoted to him. He was no doubt feeling lonely and there you were looking lovely and lonely too, but I'm sure when he gets home he will see he has been making an ass of himself. I think the whole thing sounds barmy.'

She looked at me murderously. 'I knew you wouldn't understand. He's not a bit like that.' 'He's honest and decent, you'd know that the moment you met him. Anyway it's all fixed and I'm to fly out in July. He bought the tickets and booked the seats.'

She turned away in sulky defiance. My heart sank. Here we were in late April and by June the season would be in full swing. How on earth was I going to replace her in two months?

'Can't Peter come down here and we could talk things over?' I began...

But she chipped in, 'No, he can't come here. I don't vant you poking your nose in. I'd like you to see how vonderful he is, but I don't vant you dragging in all that moral stuff about vives and children. You're a prig, that's your trouble.' She marched off in a fury.

I couldn't really see why sympathy for an unknown and shortly to be deeply hurt wife should be considered as priggish. I knew Gerdy would have been completely shattered if her marriage had been broken up in this way. She would have been the first to fight for security for herself and the children.

For the next few days we alternated between bouts of strained politeness and sullen silence and then she disappeared for a few days, presumably to say goodbye to Peter.

She returned looking sad but triumphant and waved three pink air tickets under my nose. Her departure was fixed for June 30th. Her moods thereafter relied entirely on letters. Some days they arrived in solid reassuring packs and all was sparkling gaiety, but when several days went by without even a postcard, she would mooch around, despondent and bad tempered. I found myself swinging with her, and this being contagious, the whole household tended to swing all unknowing with us. It was an uneasy time.

One morning a particularly solid letter arrived. Gerdy, grabbing it eagerly, went to her room. I was used by now to her disappearances but this was longer than most. Eventually I found her sobbing, almost hysterical, lying on her bed with sheets of the letter scattered in all directions.

I wasn't feeling particularly sympathetic as it was nearly lunchtime. It was Brenda's day off, so one of us would have to collect and clean up the children whilst the other helped Cookie in the kitchen, who was 'all behind' as usual. However, this was obviously a crisis. If she was going to be of the slightest use, I would have to listen and prod her back into some sort of shape.

'Whatever is the trouble,' I murmured, sitting down beside her, while trying to keep the irritation out of my voice. 'Cheer up old thing, it can't be as bad as it seems.'

My hope was that it was far worse than it seemed and all this nonsense with Peter would come to an end, so we could settle back into the old routine.

'Peter's written to tell me that it's all off,' she sobbed. 'He feels he can't leave his vife and he says she's been a good vife for all these years, so he doesn't vant to hurt her. He thinks the children need him and he has decided not to do anything drastic until they are grown up and standing on their own feet.'

'Good' I thought 'It's just as I had hoped. He's got some sense after all.'

'Oh bad luck Gerdy,' I paused, and then asked as briskly as I dared, 'What made him decide so soon?'

Time was racing on and this looked as though it was going to be a prolonged session.

'Read the letter,' she wailed giving an impatient shrug. I crawled around picking up the scattered pages; noting with relief that the sensible chap had numbered them. I read in silence. Though appreciating the blow this must have been for Gerdy, as the discarded woman, my heart approved of Peter's good sense and loyalty. He had returned to find a loving wife waiting to welcome him. A lovely dinner party with all his best friends had been arranged, with his two boys bouncing round devotedly. He realised his affair with Gerdy had been a wonderful fantasy. He loved her dearly, he'd never ever forget her, but he felt ashamed for causing her this sadness as he knew he'd been a brute, but he also knew that she was far too fine a character to be happy knowing that she had come between a man and his faithful wife etc.

Apart from going on and on rather, it was a splendid letter. I grew quite attached to him before I was halfway through. It was full of all the right sentiments. Any wife would be proud of such a husband. He ended by asking her if she would accept the price of the tickets as this was only some small way in which he could show his gratitude for the happiness she had given him.

Poor Gerdy. I patted her shoulder sympathetically. 'How awful for you. I do feel sorry my dear. What a brute he is to treat you like this.'

I wondered desperately how long I dared spend on this drama. I could hear the children trailing up the stairs. It sounded as though they were dragging half the beach with them, as well as several stray children and something that sounded suspiciously like a donkey in distress.

'Terrible, terrible,' I murmured as my patting became more frantic. Gerdy wailed distractedly and I could see she was in no state to cope with children or with lunch.

'I'll get you a stiff gin. You just lie there and grieve.' This I felt was magnanimous, but she was far past noticing. She just moaned throwing herself from side to side in a desperate fashion.

When I returned with the gin I was relieved to see a slight change. She was sitting up, looking sodden but oddly determined. I had innocently assumed that discarded women wept, ground their teeth and then gradually recovered, picking up the threads of their shattered lives, but I had not reckoned on such a rapid change. She glared at me as she thumped the bed.

'He can't shake me off as easily as this,' she shouted. 'Accept the price of those tickets, not jolly likely. I'm going to get out there and MAKE him marry me. He promised and he shall stick to his promise'.

'Gerdy you're being idiotic. You can't burst into a man's life and make him do anything. If he wants to keep his marriage together he'll do just that. All you'll do is make a beastly scandal.'

'I don't care, I love him and I'm determined to get him.'

'You don't love him, you can't,' I yelled. 'If you loved him you'd want his happiness and the happiness of his family. You're just being damned selfish.'

She turned on me so fiercely, I was afraid. She threw a book wildly in the direction of my head and then burst into tears.

After a short pause, which gave her long enough to draw breath, she said with desperation, 'I don't know if I love him or not, all I know is that I can't stand this hell-hole another moment. I hate this life. I hate all those horrible people and all those horrible meals. I loathe having to vork so hard in this second rate beastly little town.'

'This seedy hotel, this miserable life vith not enough money for pretty clothes or school fees or anything. I vant to give my children a decent life, not cheap dreary second best things. I hate never having time to play with them or even getting to know them properly. I vant to be a proper mother. I don't care if I am selfish. Men shouldn't die and leave their vidows to struggle and fight all on their own. I married so as to be protected and loved. It's not fair that I should be left on my own. If I can't have Peter as a husband, then he'll jolly well have to keep me as his mistress. I'm finished with this dreary respectable life of grind, grind and more grind. Indians have the right idea ven they burn the widows on the funeral pyre. This is an impossible life and I'm going to change it right now.'

'But that's immoral Gerdy. If you lived with him for love, well that's one thing. I suppose you could justify it, but what you're planning is to live with Peter simply because you're fed up with hard work and lack of money. I don't think you will get happiness that way,' I said doubtfully, none too sure of my ground. Perhaps mistresses did, but what about the children. It would put them in an invidious position wouldn't it?

'My dear Kirstine you don't know a thing about life do you? You think because you read a lot of sloppy books, because people talk a lot of nonsense about love that women marry men and live vith them because they love them. Nine times out of ten they marry because they have maneuvered, or been maneuvered by their clever Mamas, into getting a secure home. They live with them for much the same reason. You're a prig and a prude, but worse than that you're credulous, ignorant and very stupid.'

'You believe implicitly that the reasons people give for doing things are genuine. Practically everyone has different motives from those they admit to. At least I'm being honest when I say I cannot stomach this life one moment longer. You're a prig and you'll remain a prig in this dreary hole, because you don't know any better.'

'You like these dull respectable people. I hate them. You think this beastly little hotel is vonderful, but it's bourgeois and ordinary. It means nothing to me but vork, vork, vork.'

She was venomous. And I was blazing.

'You call me a prude, but there was no talk of that when principles had to be thrown overboard in order to get this place started. You were glad enough to have me go out to get what I could on the black market. You needed to eat to live then. You were glad enough to have me do all the risky dirty work.' I stopped for breath.

'There was no talk then about wanting to be a proper mother when you were swanning around the Waldorf amongst all those phony cocktail drinkers. You've allowed yourself to be fooled by that place and it's turned your silly head.' I was nearly in tears.

'Vell, I don't need you now, but before I go I vant to take out the money I put into this potty little business. I vant my £2000, so you'd better set about raising it right now. You haven't got long, so you'd better get cracking.'

She stared at me her eyes as cold as iced tea, then her glance wavered and she turned away.

'But Gerdy,' I began then saw that anything I could say would be useless. We were both so angry, far past thinking rationally. I went downstairs feeling hurt and deeply shocked, bewildered too. Was I priggish, smug, credulous, and ignorant? Was this really a dreary seedy little hotel? Were all our guests dull and bourgeois? If they were, was this relevant? It fed and housed us. A cold sense of desolation overwhelmed me. How on earth was I going to raise £2000 in under two months?

Gloomily that evening I tried to puzzle things out. Was I shocked at Gerdy's plans because they inconvenienced me personally or was it jealousy at the thought of her escaping with a wonderful lover? Was she perhaps right to determine by fair means or foul to have some sort of normal life with her children? Were they suffering because of the hectic life we led?

I thought of a friend, another widow who only that week had committed suicide on the very day her little boy started school. She left a letter saying she could not face the blank loneliness of her days without him. Having invested all of herself in the child, she was bereft without him by her side all of the time. I watched Nick and Adrian teetering precariously along the garden wall, the girls issuing shrill unheeded instructions from the middle of a flower bed. I had to admit they looked neither sad nor neglected. I knew remonstrations from me, however lovingly given, would be regarded as unwanted interference. Perhaps better a live abstracted mother than a dead possessive one, I mused sadly. It was all too complicated to work out now, but where was I going to find that £2000?

Unable to sleep that night I went out. The air was crisp and refreshing; the sky glittering with stars and the moon's path silvery gold on a sea wrinkled like silk. A cool breeze fanned my burning cheeks. The only sound was the soft murmuring of gentle waves on shingle. The water rippled over my bare feet. I stood, hardly thinking until the sky became milky white and I could see Dawlish Warren floating in a pale mist.

It was dawn, another day and time to tackle the horrendous task of raising Gerdy's £2000.

Chapter 16

April 1950 – Broken Dreams

The next day I went to see the Bank Manager, no longer the kind understanding Mr. Gliddon who had taken such a gamble in lending us the £5,500. He had died of a heart attack the previous year. Now a stout morose man sat before me, tight mouthed, stony faced, with shrewd steely eyes glinting coldly. I told him briefly what had happened and asked point blank if he would lend a further £2,000. I told him nothing about Peter; simply that Gerdy had grown tired of the hotel and wanted to start a new life in Australia. He listened without comment then sent for an enormous balance sheet. My heart sank as it always did when figures were produced. He studied the columns then looked at me severely.

'I'm afraid Mrs. Richards these figures do not justify a further loan. I will of course put the matter before Head Office if you wish, but I would not advise it. Already they have been asking why the overdraft has been reduced by so little.'

'As you know, when this loan was made three years ago, a loan which in my considered opinion was very inadvisable, you and Mrs. Ramsay promised to reduce it by £1,000 a year. So far you have only repaid slightly over £900, little over £300 a year. This is not good enough. My advice to you is to sell the place as soon as you can.'

'But Mr. Canny, I know I can make it pay if I'm given time. These first years have been very difficult. There has been so much to buy, everything costs so much. Now that Mrs. Ramsay is leaving I shall have two more rooms to let – no, three,' I corrected myself. 'As you know each room brings in about £1,000 a year. Out of this extra £3,000 I know I can make enough to pay back the loan. I aim to convert two outhouses into chalets for my children. With only two I shan't need a child minder. Anyway Brenda is getting married soon so will be leaving'.

He brightened a little and admitted grudgingly, 'That certainly makes things look a bit better but I must warn you that our policy is not to lend money to women in business on their own. With this I am in full agreement.'

'Why ever not?' I demanded indignantly. 'I should have thought that a woman with young children is one of the better risks. She dare not fool around. All the women I know work far harder than most men. One only needs to look at the local hotels, the wives work non-stop behind the scenes whilst their husbands stand around talking to the guests. Anyway how on earth are widows with children supposed to manage if they're not helped by banks?'

He gave a condescending smile which said clearly 'The answer lies in your own hands – find another husband.' I sat there seething.

'I will certainly put it to Head Office but don't raise your hopes too high.' He was cold and distant as he bowed me out of the office. I could sense he had no intention of putting my case fairly to the directors.

Within three days I received a letter telling me that they were not willing to increase the overdraft.

What should I do now? A Building Society? Yes, that was the idea, so with hope battling with despair I drove into Exeter. 'Certainly Madam, we shall be glad to view the property' said a brisk young man. 'Where did you say it was? Exmouth, splendid. An up and coming seaside resort. Which day would be convenient?'

'How about tomorrow,' I suggested, feeling cheered by the interest he was showing.

'Certainly. How about 11.00 am? Would that time suit your husband?'

'11.00 am would be perfectly convenient' I told him. 'But I haven't got a husband. I'm a widow.'

'A widow Madam. I'm sorry to hear that.' There was a marked fall in the temperature. 'A widow you say. I'm afraid this makes quite a difference. But perhaps your father... or maybe a brother...? You see Madam, we don't really like lending to ladies in business on their own.'

'But surely a widow with dependents is a splendid risk. You must know she will work her fingers to the bone.'

But he shook his head sadly, mumbling were it left to him he would of course help single ladies but it was the policy of the Abbey National etc, etc.

'But surely you will come and look at the place?' I pleaded. 'I'm sure once you've seen it you wouldn't have any doubts about lending this money'.

He grudgingly agreed to send Mr. Jones to inspect but warned me not to be too hopeful.

Mr. Jones came and enigmatically measured everything. The next day a curt note arrived saying the Abbey National was unable to help.

I then tried the Provincial and was met there by blank refusal.

'Under no circumstances do we consider lending money to a business run by a woman on her own.'

I tried the Bristol and West who said, 'We never lend to unsupported women.' I thought bitterly that that rules women out altogether, for if they are supported they presumably don't need to borrow. I was getting desperate.

At the Halifax I fared a little better. A spry elderly man arranged to come with a surveyor. Of course they chose a terrible day with a gale howling off the sea hurling great angry walls of rain directly at all the windows. This South West wind, bringing a deluge came seldom, but when it did we philosophically sat it out placing rolled towels along the window ledges, putting buckets in strategic places. Then we avoided as much as possible the huddle of miserable guests glaring from every draughty corner.

Mr. Leger's face grew longer and longer as we moved from room to room. I tried to pass him off as a prospective holiday maker, but his discreet tapping of walls and inspection of chimney breasts exploded that subterfuge. Sullen families crouched round spitting gas fires, gazed with suspicion as we prodded our way round. Babies howled, toddlers screamed, I had never seen my poor Seagull look so dilapidated. It was no surprise to receive a letter the following day saying a second mortgage could not be arranged.

Feeling deflated I contacted our lawyer, but he took the same line as Mr. Canny. The business was not really a worthwhile project. He considered I would be well advised to find a buyer and clear out. But then what would I do?

I would never be able to raise money again for another venture. I dreaded a return to working for other people, even worse, living in other people's houses. It was no life for the children and horrible for me. Now, just when the hotel was becoming known and with three extra rooms to let, I could at last see the possibility of making it pay. If we sold now all the tremendous hard work in getting the place established would benefit someone else. At this time more and more of our visitors were returning each year and recommending us to their friends. We were also gaining quite a reputation for serving good food. With a table license I knew I could build up that side of the business for local people.

However, there seemed no alternative. Reluctantly I contacted an estate agent. He was eager for business but he too chose to visit on a sour dismal day. It was obvious he thought little of our efforts. Everything wilted under his critical gaze and by the time he had completed his tour I could see the price we had hoped to get had dropped by thousands. He took a gloomy view of even finding a buyer, laughing scornfully when Gerdy told him she wanted a quick sale as she had to be out within six weeks.

'You've lost the Spring market,' he explained. 'Hotels and boarding houses sell in the early·Spring so that buyers have the season ahead. Even if we found someone tomorrow, which is highly unlikely, you would certainly not get your money for several months. Solicitors and surveyors have to be consulted, contracts have to be drawn up and exchanged. These negotiations would in all probability still be going on well into September.'

Gerdy looked mutinous, muttering, 'I have to have my £2,000 by 30th June vatever happens.'

Mr. Dougherty pricked up his ears. 'If you are thinking of a very quick sale and don't mind how little you get for the place why not put it up for auction? You might get an offer,' but he looked doubtful.

Appalled, I shouted, 'No, we must wait to get as good a price as possible. We've got the bank loan to payoff. We simply must get a price well above that, if we're going to get anything out of it for ourselves.'

'Don't forget Gerdy all our furniture has been swallowed up in this place. I can't afford to lose everything, neither can you, so please don't be idiotic.'

'I think that's a very good idea:' said Gerdy,' turning to Mr. Dougherty. 'Ve can put a minimum price on it, I suppose £10,000 at least.'

He shook his head sucking in his lips, 'Very doubtful but we can try.' He made a few notes and stumped off.

A few days later two businesslike men arrived and started sticking little tickets on all the furniture. It was like a horrible nightmare. I couldn't believe it was happening, that perhaps in a few weeks I should be homeless, answering advertisements, searching for some dreary job that accepted children. The thought of going back to that life made me feel desperate.

Our doctor who was visiting one of the guests found me nearly in tears.

'Cheer up Kirstine,' he said patting my back kindly. 'Nothing is ever as bad as it seems. What's the trouble?'

'Gerdy is leaving,' I sobbed.

'I know, you told me that last time I came. She's going out to Australia isn't she? Lucky devil, I wish I were. When does she go?'

'But it means we have to put the hotel up for sale' I blurted out. 'She needs the money she put into it. I can't raise a second mortgage so it has got to be auctioned.'

He looked shocked. 'Oh she'd never do that. Why she knows it's your bread and butter, it's a wonderful place. There's nothing like it for miles around. Of course she won't put it under the hammer.'

'But you don't understand. You really don't,' I wailed. 'Come and look in the dining room. There are two horrid men in bowler hats sticking tickets all over everything. Come and see.'

In amazement the good doctor stood staring. 'Well. I never would have believed it. Whatever has got into the girl?' He went off shaking his head in bewilderment.

I had always been able to snatch some lighthearted moments even when things were bad, but now all was despair as I thought desperately of ways in which I could save my little Seagull. I seemed to be hanging on day by day with tightly clenched teeth unable to think of anything other than raising that wretched £2000.

Gerdy and I did our work, taking the children to the beach every afternoon, but apart from commenting on the kids we hardly spoke at all.

It was a wretched time. Mr. O'Brien, our accountant, instructed by the frightening Mr. Barclay, arrived in early May and spent two or three days going through the year's figures. On being told of Gerdy's plans he looked grave and a little sad. He enjoyed these brief spells away from stuffy London, always accompanied by his wife and daughter, appearing to find our haphazard book-keeping amusing rather than irritating. Sometimes he told us we'd made a profit, sometimes a loss, but it was all profit to me when I looked at the full tummies and rosy cheeks of the children.

On leaving he squeezed my hand murmuring sympathetically. 'Mr. Barclay isn't going to like this. He's due back from Canada next week. I shall tell him your news. He takes a great interest in this little venture. He always felt sure you would make a success of it one day. I shall tell him the true position of course. He'll be sorry I know.'

I couldn't picture Mr. Barclay's sorrow. He had given the impression that he thought The Seagull a rather bad joke. Any interest he had shown was, I felt sure, because of affection for nice Mr. Gliddon. No, I certainly could not think of Mr. Barclay grieving over The Seagull. For one thing he was usually at the other side of the world meeting millionaires, for the other he still terrified me. He occasionally swooped down from London and strutted about trying to ring non-existent bells, demanding double whiskies in the middle of the children's bath time. He poked his nose into everything, still thought we ought to budget more efficiently, but praised our cooking and liked the decor. He made sour faces over the bathrooms which we had created with such difficulty, but was kind enough to say we could make a decent profit if we just 'stuck at it', but his look suggested that women seldom 'stuck at anything' and here was Gerdy justifying his cynical foreboding. The only person who was totally unaffected by his awe inspiring presence was Cookie, who bossed him around in her usual high-handed manner if ever he strayed across her path.

I found him carrying a tray of puddings from kitchen to pantry on one of her more frenzied evenings. He looked a bit astounded but ever after enquired most tenderly after 'that remarkable sister of yours,' and never failed to take her a large double gin which was more than he did for Gerdy and me. No, I couldn't picture Mr. Barclay's sorrow.

But these words from Mr. O'Brien were the first real comfort I had as only he knew the full facts. I hesitated to tell our mutual friends the true situation, there was so much that could not be told and without the whole story it made little sense. I found that when the men I had consulted were not able to help they tended to be brusque. I suppose they were frightened of becoming emotionally involved so brushed aside the human problem completely. This had the effect of making me feel guilty in having a human problem at all, so I hid my anxiety beneath a mask of indifference while being conscious of a deep sense of failure.

It had been a relief to talk openly to Mr. O'Brien knowing he understood how serious the situation was.

A day or so later a telegram arrived from Mr. Barclay, 'Reserve room one night, arriving 6.00 pm.'

I was stunned. Whatever could Mr. Barclay be coming for? He arrived with all the brisk bustle of a successful tycoon, his footfalls heavy as he stamped through the hall issuing orders, scattering children in his wake. Anything less like a carefree holiday maker was hard to imagine. As I showed him to his room I tried to assess whether my dislike of him outweighed my unwilling admiration. He so obviously and insolently didn't give a damn for anyone, despising our nice guests, spotting every flaw in the paintwork, yet there was some quality in him which compelled my unwilling respect. Sardonic, shrewd, ruthless, his quick brain clarified my muddled thinking and I always found him stimulating.

'We'll talk after dinner,' he said brusquely. No request whether this would be convenient, simply a flat command.

'Well, what's this I hear?' He was looking at me with penetrating appraisal as I handed him a large brandy.

He listened without comment until I finished, then said, 'I think Gerdy is doing the wise thing. She was never suited to this life. You realise of course she is much more of a realist than you. She can see clearly this place for what it is, she also knows the break was bound to come eventually so is sensibly cutting her losses.'

I hadn't expected sympathy but neither had I expected him to take Gerdy's side so completely.

'But what's going to happen to me and the children?' I demanded in astonished outrage. He shrugged, adopting a lofty pompous attitude.

'That's quite beside the point. The point is that you want to hang on to an unprofitable business which entails too much work for the reward it brings. This is unrealistic. To put it under the hammer is also unrealistic. I cannot see any point in rushing things like this, but no doubt Gerdy has her reasons.' He looked at me enquiringly, eyes morose under tufted brows, sharply intelligent, missing nothing.

I could see he would not be satisfied until he had heard the whole story, so as briefly as possible I outlined her plans.

'Yes, I can see now why she is in such a hurry but that's no good reason for ruining you. But putting that aside do you really want to go on running this place on your own?'

I took a deep quivering breath. 'Yes, I do. I can't bear the thought of giving it all up after these three grinding years especially when it is on the edge of success. Every stick of furniture, every lick of paint was fought for inch by inch. It may look tacky to you but to me it's a beautiful miracle. The guests may all look very ordinary but to me they are interesting appreciative human beings. When they praise us for what we do I glow with pride. The staff may seem amateurish and a bit ropey to you but to me they are my friends. I love every inch of the place with all its shortcomings and handicaps. It will break my heart if I have to give it up and start all over again.'

He looked at me speculatively for several moments, then to my astonishment said, 'Right, I'll give you a cheque for £2000.

You can get rid of Gerdy right away. She doesn't deserve it, she'd get a good deal less if you put it up for auction, but this will settle one part of your problems.'

With that he wrote out a cheque and handed it to me.

I gasped, stuttered, than managed to blurt out, 'This is fantastically kind of you. I don't know how to thank you. Of course I'll pay you back. I want it to be a completely business-like deal.' I tried hard through my confusion to look business-like and efficient.

He looked at me sardonically saying nothing whilst I babbled on. Then he leant forward and said quietly his dark eyes sparkling with something that looked like malice.

'What do I get out of this?'

'Why, what do you mean?' I stammered. 'Naturally I will pay you interest, I mean to pay you back long before I pay anything to that silly bank.'

His eyes contracted, the pupils dilated, then with satiric irony, 'Don't be so naive Kirstine. If I want to invest money I don't choose potty little seaside hotels. I'm not talking of money. I'm talking about you and me. What do I get out of it?' He sat back and waited with a cynical smile on his lips, his whole posture one of sharp intentness.

I knew what he meant and flung the cheque across the table as though it had stung me. Quietly he picked it up, folded it in two and placed it carefully in his pocket book. I looked at him blankly. My mind flickered back to the starchy hospital matron, her cold 'You could be sure of taking home £4.00 each week.' I remembered the horror of that awful school where I'd first heard of Gerry's death, where the greedy head mistress had suggested that in exchange for my services, she would educate the children.

I remembered her lies, her exploitation of anyone she could get in her power. I thought of the miserable room I had shared with the children whilst waiting for an idea to materialise which would make us independent of other people's homes and peculiar habits. I thought of the terrible discomfort of my eccentric mother's house. Could I make any of these our future? Were my children to be doomed to grow up barely tolerated in other people's surroundings with me nervous, irritable and chained by drudgery? Had I to return to the fear of exploitation and lack of privacy which is the lot of most widows? What we had here was that most precious of all gifts, 'freedom', I could not give it up.

Once long ago this man had said. 'Everyone has their price. It's just a question of finding out what that price is.' I had been indignant.

He was watching me closely. I hesitated, then with a nervous half smile I held out my hand. Without a word he took out his pocket book, unfolded the cheque placing it on my open palm. It crackled as I fingered it.

Was this my price? Were morals like principles? Expensive luxuries,which could be discarded, when things got too tough. It was ironic that Gerdy's lapse from moral rectitude was to enable her to get away from The Seagull, mine to enable me to stay. Who could judge which one of us had the better case, or had we any case at all?

The silence was only disturbed by the soft ticking of the clock and the gentle swish of the lapping waves on the shore. Glancing up I caught an odd speculative look in his eyes which I could not interpret. His swarthy skin shone dark in the evening dusk, his expression was downright wicked. Blast the man, why should he corner me like this? Looking at his inscrutable face I tried to follow his motives. If he wants to help then why can't he do it in a straightforward manner instead of playing cat and mouse in this maddening way? I could almost see his tail flick. Was there lurking amusement behind that calculating look? I needed his beastly money desperately but I was damned if I was going to be maneuvered into a false position.

I had offered a sensible business proposition. Even if he did think The Seagull a wretched concern, this would be just as good a proposition, if I paid the proper rate of interest, as it would have been had he lent the money to The Savoy Hotel.

Gazing at the cheque as it lay in my hand I pondered, then looking straight at him said carefully,

'For one moment I thought you were serious, but now I can see you're too honourable to take advantage of my position. I will gladly accept your loan giving you in return my heartfelt gratitude and my friendship, if this is of any value.'

His look changed first to surprise, then amusement. He lay back in his chair and laughed outright. This was the last reaction I had expected. I didn't think it very flattering. What an aggravating man I thought, looking at him coldly, I couldn't see that I had said anything particularly funny.

After several minutes he straightened his tie, wiped his eyes and said weakly,

'Kirstine, Kirstine what a girl you are. I'd back you anywhere and they say women are the weaker sex.'

Then seeing me fingering the cheque doubtfully his tone altered, 'Take it my dear. 6% is the correct rate of interest. I'll have them send you a quarterly bill. I shall expect to be paid back in full.' His tone changed to one of simple friendliness,

'You know Kirstine you haven't done at all badly. For a small business to carry six, seven if you count that pretty nurse girl, and make a profit each year, even if it is a very small one, that isn't bad going. You should do very well on your own without Gerdy. But as I said before, Gerdy is much more of a realist than you. I understand her motivation but I'm damned if I understand yours.'

'How?' I asked bristling.

'How? Well, Gerdy isn't prepared to go on working like a slave if she can find someone to support her in comfort. Now you – what makes you tick I wonder?' He looked at me quizzically.

I pondered. I didn't know, yet perhaps I did. Wasn't it the challenge that for me gave life it's zest? Without it I was bored. I had enjoyed being married. The companionship and the warmth of two people who were closely tied by their love for each other and for their children. The physical side of marriage was delicious, but I'd missed the fight and the struggle, the pitting of my wits and strength against all odds. Married and secure I had not felt stretched. Certainly Gerry had been fighting to get established in the practice, to become recognised as a good doctor, but it hadn't been my fight. I'd been on the sidelines, merely an observer, always feeling that I was on the edge of where the action was. So perhaps all this had nothing to do with morals, mine or Gerdy's. Her decision was made because the uncertainty and insecurity of this life was for her intolerable; mine was made because for me the certainty and security were equally intolerable.

We had both got what we needed because we were the kind of people we were.

I had a desire to laugh loudly, wildly and in so doing snap the nervous tension of the last hour. The clock ticked on quietly and Mr. Barclay waited, as I reflected. Then smiling I clicked on the light fetched a bottle of Niersteiner and we drank companionably to the future success of The Seagull. I found the frightening Clifford Barclay far less fearsome, a great deal more understanding than I had imagined. That night we cemented a close, though prickly friendship that lasted for years.

It was only after I had crept into bed hours later faint with exhaustion that I saw the funny side of this weird encounter. As I lay weakly giggling, I realised fully for the first time that The Seagull was safe. It was mine now, it rested with me alone to make it a success, to show that a woman on her own was worth backing. It was up to me to convince those supercilious men who had so calmly promoted women's role as that of dependence on the whim of others.

'I'll show them' I muttered sleepily. 'The Seagull will be the best hotel this side of Salisbury'.

Never mix business with pleasure. Well, both were inextricably mixed to my mind. My business should be well spiced with enjoyment, my pleasure well laced with resolution. With that I fell asleep.

Chapter 17

The Parting

So Gerdy left. I was on my own. In those last few weeks I longed to patch up our quarrel, tell her I understood how she felt, that she was right to go, but the rift was too great, too recent for reconciliation. I was hesitant as well because I dreaded that she might change her mind, decide to stay. Letters from Australia had ceased to arrive. I knew she was becoming increasingly anxious as the date of departure drew near. I felt torn knowing that The Seagull could never have prospered with her discontent pervading everything. It would have been a situation where decisions which ought to be made would be stalled, then made too late or in the wrong sequence, thus causing confusion for guests and staff alike.

Just once we had drawn near when with doubt in her eyes and uncertainty in her manner she had asked. 'Am I doing the right thing Kirstine?' For the first time in my life I had given what I knew in my heart (or thought I knew) to be bad advice.,'If you want to get that man Gerdy you get out there good and fast.'

I had one more bad scare when Brenda said casually, 'I thought Gerdy was taking the children with her when she leaves.'

'Of course she is,' I answered, 'they all leave together on the 16th – their passage is booked.'

'But I've just been talking with her,' said Brenda puzzled,

'She's been explaining to me about which clothes they are to wear next winter.'

'Oh you must have misunderstood. She probably meant which clothes she wanted you to pack but there she is now, I'll find out what she meant.'

'Gerdy,' I called, 'You are taking the children with you – you're not planning on leaving them here. Brenda seems to have got a bit muddled.'

There was consternation in her eyes which she swiftly masked, then after a slight pause said

'No, I'm not taking them. I've decided I can't possibly start a new life with them round my feet all the time. I will send for them later when I've got established.'

She coloured, looking defiant, so pretty in her midcalf 'new look' dress with its neat waist and swirling bunchy skirt.

In stunned disbelief I replied, 'But Gerdy you can't do that! The only possible way I can pay back that £2000 I've borrowed is by letting every available inch of space. If Adrian and Christel stay then I have to keep Brenda on or replace her – that's two bedrooms lost. You simply must take them as planned.'

The flush paled from her cheeks, her small firm chin set more stubbornly.

'Vat can I do!, she wailed plaintively,' my hands vill be completely tied if I have to look after them. I shall have to find vork as soon as I get there. How can I manage in a strange country on my own?' frightened eyes stared into mine.

'What about my hands being tied. I've landed myself with this extra horrible debt on the strict understanding that I'd have those rooms. You know I'd never have got this loan if Clifford had known about this. Anyway, what about the children, how will they feel if you leave them, and how do I know if you will ever send for them? No, I'm sorry,' My voice hardened 'You will have to take them or make other arrangements. Couldn't you send them to your parents in Bonne – surely they'd love to have their grandchildren?'

She stiffened, 'That's impossible. You know they lost everything in the war. They are now living in a cramped one-bedroomed flat with barely enough room for themselves. Mami is not at all vell. I've already asked them – they say it's impossible.'

'What about your sister in Brazil – she's got an enormous house in Rio?' 'I don't want them brought up by Christa – her children are spoilt over-indulged brats.'

'Well, it looks to me as though you are going to have to choose one or the other or take them with you – you are not leaving them here.'

I walked away hating myself for being so mean but knew if I gave in I'd never repay the £2000. I'd never get my head above water. Much as I loved Christel and Adrian I knew if I became responsible for them as well as my two we'd all go under.

When the day arrived for their departure, we said goodbye wordlessly with only the children expressing our grief, for they were genuinely sad. As I turned away from the taxi my eyes were filled with tears, my heart a curious mixture of guilt, desolation and elation. We'd tackled so much together; had so much fun, shared so much sorrow. Would she be alright with the children in a strange country on her own? Had I been right to insist that she take them with her? I was free at last, could look forward to a less complicated life without the nagging worry of Gerdy's unhappiness, but should I have tried to help her more. Perhaps if we'd been older and wiser this impasse need never have arisen I thought sadly as I tried to console Lu who had already sensed what the loss of her friends would mean.

'I wonder what Adrian's doing now. Will Christel come back?' was her constant refrain for many months but gradually she became adjusted. Nick, absorbed in his own world, took the parting less hard.

CHAPTER 18

MOVING ON

Whilst we at The Seagull were endeavouring to get established, Exmouth was enduring similar difficulties in coming to grips with the complexities of peace. Still shaken by the 1943 bombing of the town centre there now raged ongoing battles between those who wanted the little seaside town to become a popular go-ahead resort rivalling Minehead with fun fairs, charabancs, dodgems and day trippers, and those equally determined it should return to the golden days of genteel elegance.

Gerdy and I in our own small way had symbolised Exmouth's dilemma. As professional men's widows we qualified to become members of the exclusive Exmouth Club. As hoteliers 'in trade' we did not, thus causing committee discord. By the time we were voted in by a majority of one, we were far too busy to use the club. Even so we felt that we had scored a point by becoming the thin edges of a wedge of progress for working widows.

The first defeat or victory, depending on where one's sympathy lay, was when a row of charming old coast guard cottages were demolished, a children's playground put in their place. Despite strong opposition the windy sand-swept golf course was re-established as a public right of way, much to the delight of dog lovers, bird watchers and picnickers, while the club house became a small zoo.

There were some who vigorously opposed Southlands School becoming a teacher training college, later Rolle College, even though this gave trade a welcome boost.

Possibly the most valuable asset was when a professional theatre company made Exmouth its headquarters becoming one of the most respected repertory companies in the country. Many youngsters, like Joan Plowright, made their debut with the Exmouth Theatre Co, under the direction of Joyce and John Worsley.

The development of the Pavilion caused further controversy. The orchestral concerts given daily could have been a success had management shown imagination, but hard upright chairs arranged in regimented rows, self service refreshments slopping about on tin trays and the counter staff's chattering, did nothing to enhance the spirit of the occasion. Tentative suggestions of 'thé dansant' were met with abhorrence although these might have proved popular with holidaymakers in bad weather.

Another row broke out when a delegation from the council pleaded for a refuse destructor. This was vigorously opposed by Ministry of Health officials determined that tipping should continue – Woodbury Common to be used for this purpose. Fortunately they were over-ruled and the town got its destructor. Apart from the marine's well camouflaged assault course, Woodbury Common's beauty remained undisturbed.

With the lifting of restrictions a boom in house building began. The average price for a comfortable three bedroom house was £1650. The post war years 1946 to 1952 was a time of progress despite fierce opposition.

Meanwhile we at The Seagull had attracted several misfits in the dining room after Leslie left. Kazimir, a taciturn melancholy man, seeming to carry all of Poland's tragic history on his sunken shoulders, entered our lives briefly. He hated taking orders from women, disliked the British (holiday makers in particular) viewed children with distaste and served at table haughtily. As he'd been studying law when Germany invaded Poland his resentment was understandable, but this didn't radiate much jollity. Though in no way a frivolous man he did wear a pink hairnet at bedtime so he must have had a softer side to his sombre nature. How he had been washed up in Exmouth remained as mysterious as his gloomy personality. Unexpectedly he produced a timid and very pregnant wife who spoke no English. Ignored by Kazimir Maria crept about trying to be helpful, her enormous stomach defeating this laudable intention, her wistful 'pleas, pleas' tugging at our over-stretched heartstrings.

Not many days after her arrival Kazimir woke me, pink hairnet coquettishly draped over one distracted eye,

'Madame, Madame. The babee it com – you com – queek, queek'

Maria's yells made this all too obvious.

Fortunately our doctor had arranged for the birth to take place at the house of a retired nurse. Confused by Maria's screams I inadvertently drove down the wrong road – a cul de sac – and was deeply embarrassed as lights popped on in every window as we retraced our earsplitting course.

Kazimir, enigmatic as ever, ignoring my suggestion that he should remain with Maria to act as interpreter, sat in the car morose and disapproving, the pink hairnet at an even more rakish angle.

On visiting the following day an exhausted nurse and doctor wordlessly, triumphantly, handed me a 12lb. boy. Maria, whose screams they told me had never ceased for one instant, was sitting up in bed eating a hearty breakfast. There was no sign of the proud father.

Fortunately within weeks Kazimir moved on. I received a postcard from the Cafe Royal, which never mentioned Maria and son.

Swiss Irvin, like a handsome if irritable actor, breathed through flaring nostrils in a hostile way when anything upset him. He nurtured a passion for Brenda. After a brief but unsuccessful skirmish he was rejected and he became even more sullen. Though we all rushed to his assistance when he was hard-pressed, his unforgiving nature made it impossible for him to help others in similar difficulties. This trait, no doubt approved by Swiss trade unionists, made him unpopular at The Seagull so he didn't last long.

We struggled on, then – 'You'll be missing a treasure,' Mary's voice over the phone was persuasive. I had worked for Mary during the war in her children's nursery and we were now firm friends. I trusted her judgement yet hesitated, athough badly in need of someone responsible.

'Honestly Mary I don't want another German after this Gerdy fracas.'

She ignored this going on briskly. 'She's fully trained. she knows all about wines. She's completed a two year course in hotel management in Germany. She really is a gem. You'll be a fool if you miss this chance. By the way she's a baroness.'

'I don't care if she's a princess, I don't want a German. Anyway,' I asked suspiciously 'how come she's with you if she's hotel trained?'

'It's a long story. She's had a pretty awful time in a hotel near Tiverton. It's a bit complicated about her work permit, but she will tell you about it if you will just see her. If she doesn't get another hotel job she'll be packed straight back to Germany where the chance of getting work is non existent. They are in a bad way over there you know.' Mary sounded reproachful.

'I know they are but the last thing I need just now is a tangle with the Home Office over work permits.'

'Please Kirstine, just see her. I promise you won't regret it.'

Unwillingly I gave in promising to see the girl the next day.

It was her voice that first attracted me to Francesca. A soft, light, lilting voice with just the faintest trace of accent. Neither pretty nor plain, she looked desperately pale and strained as she sat twisting her hands nervously, eyes glazed with anxiety.

'Tell me why you left your last job. Wasn't that a bit rash? It's not easy to transfer permits from one hotel to the other you know?'

'Yes, I know' she whispered, 'but I ad to leave – eet became impossible.' She bit her lips brushing away a tear surreptitiously.

Gradually I drew from her the whole story, how the owner usually drunk, had continually tried to seduce her behind his wife's back. When she rejected this, he swore at her in front of the customers. calling her a filthy German slut, threatening to report her to the police, and have her sent back to Germany. Homesick, desperate and frightened, knowing no one she ran away. Luckily someone kind put her in touch with a social worker who passed her on to Mary. This social worker felt sure she could have the permit transferred if Francesca could find work in another hotel.

I found her gentle timidity, her transparent honesty appealing but it was with misgiving that I agreed to give her a trial. It was the best thing I ever did. Highly skilled, with a sound knowledge of every aspect of hotel work and a winning way with guests, she became a charming hostess as well as head waitress.

Not everyone can boast of a baroness as maitre d'hôte and she certainly lent a certain cachet to the dining room, but it was more than that. Francesca had a subtleness of spirit, an inward grace, attending to guests with delicacy and genuine interest. This is the beginning and the end of service and exceedingly rare. This we learnt from our gentle little baroness who stayed with us until she married six years later.

CHAPTER 19

NOVEMBER 1951 – A NIGHT-TIME PROWLER

For some weeks the young trainee June had been complaining about late night prowling footsteps around her french windows, but I had taken no notice. Young girls are always complaining about something, laddered stockings or pimples, boy friends who are too fresh, or no boy friends at all. I was a busy hotelier with better things to do than chase shadows in windy November gardens. But I had to take notice when my hairdresser, a normally dignified and reserved man, who had been taking a moonlit walk, burst into my bedroom late one night (I slept in the office-cum-sitting room on the ground floor) dramatically announcing that he had just chased a man across the lawn, only to lose him as he darted between two cars into a side road.

'It's not the first time I've seen him. He's a nasty looking brute – big, burly wearing wellington boots. He looks as though he might be one of the dockers – a rough looking customer. He's always hanging around your place.'

Sadly I realised that something would have to be done, if only to stop late night visitations from my hairdresser, who had been deeply embarrassed to find me in bed. All right in his place, I felt, but not by my bedside at close on midnight.

The next morning I told June I wanted her to come with me to the police station. On the way, she graphically described the man who had been seen hovering in the garden by one of her friends.

'He's weedy and small, wears a beret and gym shoes,' she rambled on. Philosophically I noted the difficulty we all have in describing people accurately, pitying the poor police when it came to identifying criminals.

We made our report to a phlegmatic sergeant who wrote everything down with meticulous care. 'And you say this gentleman prowls around your french-windows at about 10.00 pm then again around 11.30 Miss?'

He looked doubtfully at June, then turning to me, 'This young lady sleeps on the ground floor?' He was severe, I could see that he thought this a very bad idea with one as pretty as June.

'Has he ever tried to enter the premises miss?' 'No,' said June, 'I just hear footsteps then after a little while they go away.' The sergeant looked disappointed. We both felt it was a bit of an anticlimax. No breaking and entering, no attack, no rape, simply a few footsteps scraping on the stone path. It sounded very limp.

'I will make a report to the Inspector then let you know what we propose to do,' said the sergeant majestically. June and I shrank out feeling abashed.

That afternoon the sergeant appeared on my doorstep accompanied by an eager red headed lad who gazed at June's pretty face with admiration, and twice had to be reprimanded for inattention by his portly superior.

'My young officer is going to patrol your premises tonight Madam. I am sure you will have no further trouble from this prowling character.'

Now, I have a theory that a great more crime could be detected if policemen didn't patrol with helmets lit up like belisha beacons in the glare of every street lamp, with heavy boots ringing like jungle drums on every square of pavement.

'Wouldn't it be a good idea, that is if you really want to catch this prowler,' I murmured feeling both silly and interfering, 'to have this young constable hide in our neighbour's shrubbery? If he wore gym shoes and ordinary clothes he could move much more easily, nor would he be so obvious.'

This suggestion was received with stony silence by the sergeant, but the young man brightened visibly. I could see his thoughts racing, an exciting dash, a mighty battle, June saved from worse than death, instant promotion, glory forever. He gazed appealingly at the sergeant, but this was obviously too novel an idea to be accepted lightly.

Some hours later the phone rang, I was informed that P.C. 138 would take cover in the bushes at 9.30 pm precisely. Would I please settle myself in June's room at the same time, out of sight. Would she leave her curtains open a crack to act as a lure. Would the young lady prepare for bed in the normal manner. Feeling like Mata Hari's we prepared for action. At 9.30 precisely, armed with a book I sank on the floor behind June's bed. She undressed discreetly behind the wardrobe and started to brush her hair. Within minutes she whispered, 'He's here.' I heard the soft scrape of footsteps on the path outside. We held our breath then, in a few seconds, heard mumble, mumble, mumble, strong male voices in muffled dispute. A slight scuffle, then no more. We peeped through the curtains but saw nothing. We dashed to the phone tense with anticipation waiting for it to ring. It rang. We heard the inspector's comforting voice telling us that they had their man. He was being questioned now, it would be perfectly safe for us to go to bed. Many congratulations with thanks all round, we departed to our respective beds.

I had been reading for only about half an hour when June bounded into my room with an ashen face, eyes popping.

'He's back again' she squeaked, 'But this time he's trying to get in. I distinctly saw the handle turn. He's out for revenge' she wailed. 'It's because we told the police. I'm frightened.'

The silly girl's gone hysterical I thought. What a time to choose when everything is all over. Well, girls are silly. I went down and listened and to my amazement I could hear once again the scraping of footsteps just outside the french-windows, then, before my eyes, the handle turned gently. There was a soft decisive rattle. He DID want to get in. I shot back to the phone with visions of us all being chopped in pieces and dialled the police.

'Put me through to the Inspector at once' I yelled.

'Yes, yes, Mrs. Richards what can we do for you?' He sounded irritable.

'Do' I shouted, 'Do. You can come right round and collect that man again. He's back here prowling around, this time he's trying to get in – it must be revenge.'

I heard myself babble, 'I've never heard of such incompetence letting that fellow escape, allowing him to come straight back and terrify the life out of us like this. No wonder the country is full of crooks if this is all you police can do when you actually get a criminal in your grasp.'

There was a short silence, then 'Wait a moment Mrs. Richards. I don't understand. You say this man is back again. But he can't be I'm still questioning him. I have him here with me now.'

It took some seconds for me to register what he had said.

'Oh Inspector I am so sorry but I heard him with my own ears. I honestly did see the handle of the door turning. There really is someone trying to get into June's room.'

'We'll send our officer round right away Mrs. Richards. Now don't you worry. He will be with you within five minutes.'

June and I waited tense with strain. Too frightened to peep through the curtains, almost more scared of looking foolish should the constable come and find no one there. But we could still hear those scraping footsteps, soft rattling of the door handle. Was it all imagination? Then scuffle, scuffle, scuffle, mumble, mumble, mumble, and an astonished, though jubilant young male voice called through the french-windows,

'Open up Mrs. Richards – we've caught another one!'

June was very pretty, but two peeping Toms and an admiring police officer in one night is a good haul for even the prettiest of girls.

Chapter 20

Trainee Students

I say Boss,' said Brenda one day, 'I've had such a peculiar conversation. You know that rather odd looking man, the one with long straggly hair and a beard. He and his family go everywhere barefoot, none of them ever eat meat? Mr. Swithers I think he's called.'

I always knew when Brenda had some special tit-bit to share with me. With dimples working overtime, eyes sparkling with barely concealed mischief she cocked her pretty head to one side.

'Well, he gave me a lift into the town this morning. On the way he said, 'The Seagull is the most communist set up I've ever come across.'

Startled I gazed at Brenda in amazement. We had been called many things over the years but never communist. 'Whatever did he mean?' I exclaimed.

'I was a bit surprised and asked him to explain. He said, 'We've been at The Seagull now for almost two weeks and in all that time we cannot decide who's running the place. All the staff take such an interest that anyone of them could be the owner. Elsie welcomed us like old friends when we arrived, we see Mrs. Richards making beds, you taking the children out. Francesca runs the dining room as though it was hers. Cookie seems to boss everyone about including the guests.' He laughed having no doubt been organized into doing something he didn't expect.' Brenda giggled then went on with her story, 'We've never heard anyone giving an order yet the place appears to be run on oiled wheels. We've had such a wonderful holiday, so has everyone else and the staff seem to have enjoyed themselves as much as the guests.'

I was deeply touched by Mr. Swithers' enthusiasm but felt his accolade did not quite fit my idea of a communist state, not if one believed the tales filtering out of East Berlin.

By degrees we had settled into a steady routine with the staff dwindling to a handful of regulars in the winter, swelling with an influx of bright young students each Spring.

It seemed as though all of Europe's youngsters wanted to work in Britain in this post-war period. Just as we had not needed to advertise The Seagull after the first year, so the students returned year after year or introduced their friends. Some had endured bad wartime experiences, especially the French, Germans and Fins. I liked to think The Seagull gave them as square a deal as they gave us; hoping we helped to create a bridge of understanding between countries that had so recently been enemies.

But more than anything I wanted Nick and Lu to grow up without inbuilt prejudice, the prejudice that can so hamper people of this island race.

We had a good system. All who came could choose the number of hours they wanted to work but those hours had to be filled conscientiously.

The rest of the day was the students' own to use as they wished. In this way no one became discontented, lazy or bored. Everyone was paid top rates, plus their share of the 10% service charge. Consequently guests were met on all sides with smiling faces and willing service. The regular staff received invaluable help plus the stimulus of passing on their professional skills to youngsters eager to learn.

Belinda, a Bristol University student, settled for a six hour day. Her fiancé came too, but because my quota was full that summer he took a job in a nearby five star hotel. Preferring Belinda's company to that of the Imperial staff, as soon as breakfast had been served Peter bustled over to The Seagull, seized the hoover spending a happy morning at his beloved's side until lunch time when he returned to his hotel in time to serve the mid-day meal. A practice not unlike some of the more adventurous Royal Ballet swans who, it was rumoured, skipped over to Drury Lane to exchange places with My Fair Lady dancers.

Not only did he keep our dining room immaculate, he also kept Nick and Lu happy with an endless supply of the Imperial's disused menu cards, the back of which made splendid drawing paper. We listened with shocked relish to his tales of their four chefs' hectic Tuesdays when the meat for the entire week was boiled, broiled, roasted, then when cold, sliced and coated with gravy made from the remains of the brown windsor soup. It was then slapped in giant hot plates to be used as needed until the following Tuesday's supply of meat arrived. This presumably satisfying the AA Inspector, who gave them all those stars.

Gerard came two summers running, holding us spell-bound with stories of life at the Sorbonne. Madame, his mother, a dignified lady from Perigord had on one historic occasion spanked the two boys, who later became famous for discovering the Lascaux caves! We felt proud of this tenuous link with fame. It was through this lady that we found Martine and Marietta two delightful teenagers from Bordeaux. I lodged Martine with friends who were fascinated by this lissom red haired miss in her crisp cottons and bouffant petticoats.

Every evening at 9.00 pm sharp she appeared at their sitting room door clad in a demure ankle length nightie, then regardless of whether they had visitors or not, kissed them a polite good night. Their faith in her docility was badly shaken when they discovered she scampered upstairs, not to bed as they imagined, but to dress again hastily before clambering out of the window to enjoy the night life of Exmouth.

I soon learnt not to attempt to supervise the life of the students out of working hours, for this they rightly guarded with fierce independence. I grew adept at making myself understood in almost any language. On their first evening saying firmly.

'Now presumably you know what happens to girls who don't take care of themselves?'

'Oui Madame. Ja geneigter frau.'

'Young men will all want to lead you astray. Comprenez? Verstanden?'

'Oui Madame. Ja geneigter frau.'

'Your mother, no doubt, asks you where you're going and with whom?'

'Oui Madame,. Ja geneigter frau.'

'Well I haven't the time nor the inclination to chase you all to bed only to have you climb out of windows when my back is turned. From now on it's your responsibility, not mine, Comprenez? Verstanden?'

'Oui, Madame. Ja geneigter frau.'

And that was that. As far as I know none of them got into serious trouble. For the first few weeks they scampered about until all hours, until gradually they realized they couldn't work properly if half asleep, so began to regularize their outings in a more sensible manner.

Marietta was even prettier than Martine and if anything more flighty. Gerard's mum who visited us one summer shook her head sadly when told by Gerard of their nocturnal adventures.

In Bordeaux and Perigord she assured me, all the girls were virtuous, all were in bed by 9.00 pm. I could see she thought I failed miserably as a chaperone.

Jean, from Normandy, arrived in a cider boat winning all hearts by his charm. He gave Nick and Lu hours of free tuition as they explored the sandy coves together. He went off one day to visit a neighbouring town returning late, breathless with a tale to tell. I was entertaining a rather staid couple that evening who had been assuring me that they would never under any circumstances engage a French tutor for their children. 'Their morals you know' they kept reiterating drearily, 'One simply cannot tell with the French.'

When Jean had been introduced and suspiciously regarded by my friends, he recounted his day's adventures, then added.

'I vass vaiting for ze buss and along came Meester Green een ees racing car' he named a young man who lived nearby.

'Ee offaired me a leeft to Exmouth, ee invite me to ees leetle ouse. C'est admirable, all peenk zatin, black lace lamps, veree veree pretee. I meet ees friend; ow do you zay ees ami? I haf nevair met wiz such a zing een France. En Angleterre zometimes. Een France nevair. Ve like ze ladees too moch.' Jean rolled his eyes in shocked delight. My friends looked pensive.

Ruth was Norwegian, a meek girl who swiftly became addicted to Devon cider and English knitting wool. Work finished for the day she perched on her bed, then knitted feverishly until midnight with a flagon of cider by her side. As far as I know she never put foot outside the hotel, but on leaving assured me gravely that she had never enjoyed a summer so much in the whole of her life.

Gigi and Eric returning one evening from a day spent in Sidmouth told me excitedly of the wonderful game they had watched whilst eating their picnic.

'Ah eet vas most indersting. Ze men zey were all in vite and zey ad a leedle ball und two leedle sticks-eet vas called 'publeec vootbath.'

Puzzled I asked them to explain.

'Yes,' they said earnestly. 'Ve zat on a zeat beside a notice vich said 'Publeec Vootbath' zo ve knew zat vas vat se game vas called.'

I doubt if our famous national game has ever been so misnamed!

Through Francesca we enjoyed a steady stream of nieces and nephews from Germany, all working industriously while playing with equal zeal. As yoga devotees Exmouth holiday-makers were edified by the sight of a row of youngsters solemnly standing on their heads by the water's edge. They could keep this up for hours and on sunny days rivalled the Punch and Judy show. Francesca, maintaining it cleared the brain and calmed the mind, was disappointed that I refrained from joining them.

Jurgen came to us first when he was eleven. Not to work but as Nick's guest in return for reciprocal hospitality. A serious child he devoted most of his waking thoughts to food.

After every meal his closely cropped head appeared round the kitchen door, and rolling his blue eyes hopefully he would say, 'Lofflee eengleesh pooding Cookie.' With any luck he would be given all the left-overs to finish.

We weren't always so fortunate with our students. Teresa, a sullen girl, arrived one Saturday and by Monday was telling each of us in turn how we should be doing our work. As she had taken a whole morning to grate and squeeze 6 oranges and 2 lemons this didn't go down well with Cookie.

'That girl will have to go she's useless.'

'Let's give her a few more days maybe she's nervous' I answered dubiously.

'Nervous, that one! I'd have put her on a charge for insolence if she'd been in my army unit. You'd best get rid of her now – she'll only get worse.'

She did get worse. The other girls didn't know what to make of her. After a few friendly overtures they shrugged and ignored her.

At the end of the week I gave her a week's notice which she met with virulence. A massive surly man came thundering down from the North, voracious for the rights of his tiresome daughter, 'Ahm a trades union official. Ah tell ye ye caant do this to ma girrl.'

'Yes I can. Teresa was appointed as a trainee on trial. She has shown clearly she has no intention of being trained.'

'Ah tell ye woman ye caant throw her att.'

'I'm not throwing her out. I've given her a week's notice but if you'd like to take her back with you, she can leave now. I will pay her for the week.'

'The girl's unhappy, she tells me all the staff are unhappy here.'

I beckoned him to the window, 'Come and look Mr. Butler.'

A bunch of youngsters were sitting in the sun, so pretty and lively in their crisp striped uniforms, laughingly struggling with a variety of languages. Blonde Ingrid from Sweden, cheeky Marietta from France, Mary's staunch little daughter Jill, lovely eccentric Mavis who walked like a queen. She sat now with her arms round her terrible dribbling bull terrier who, much to our disapproval, occupied her bed whilst she slept on the chalet floor!

'Do they look miserable?' I asked. He said nothing but his expression was clear. What can you expect from a load of foreigners who don't know any better.

'Teresa has tried hard to be disruptive but I'm happy to say she hasn't been successful.'

Mr. Butler grunted, then 'That cook of yours – she bosses ma girrl.'

'I'm not surprised. As an ex-cook sergeant she bosses all of us. Come and meet her but watch out you may find yourself stoking the Aga.'

I thought I caught a gleam of amusement in his eye.

Cookie greeted him with a roguish conspiratorial twinkle. Forthright as always she said, 'Come to take that naughty girl of yours home. I don't know what you'll do with her but a hotel is not the place for her – definitely not.'

Somewhat shaken by this he turned to me. 'Teresa says that so called baroness girl puts on airs. She doesna like it.'

'Francesca – Airs!' both of us were astounded. 'What Teresa calls airs we call good manners. But seriously Mr. Butler you've just had lunch here, would you rather be served by an untidy, sulky girl slapping plates about and scowling at you, rather than a smiling courteous Francesca? Your Teresa could learn a great deal here were she willing, but she has made it quite clear she has no desire to learn anything. She hasn't got the right attitude to work.'

They left that evening Mr. Butler looking thoughtful, Teresa still mutinous, showing clearly the virulence of her personality.

Lu, by now a boarder at Elmhurst ballet school in Camberley, helped Francesca every morning in the holidays. From quite an early age she was busily occupied polishing tables or sweeping the stairs, which led down to the dining room. This last caused me a guilty pang remembering my own hatred of this particular job as a child, but perhaps the companionship of the other youngsters made it more palatable, for I never heard any protest.

As she grew older she usually brought friends home for the holidays, they too had to do their stint, more often than not to the strains of Beethoven's Fifth, punctuated by earnest discussions on the intricacies of entrechats and pirouettes. All work ceased whilst slender and graceful they twirled around the tables, skirts flying, heads and toes held in the correct classic postures.

Rosemarie came from Berlin and was the most dramatic of all our students. She gave Nick his first serious love pangs after his return from a year at a technical school in Canada. At seventeen Rosemarie had caused her widowed mother so much concern that a psychiatrist had been consulted. He had advised travel; a long way from mother, so Rosemarie arrived on our doorstep, all seven stone of fizzing excitement and bubbling vitality. She adored rock and roll, and each evening the chalets behind the hotel shook wildly as Nick's old gramophone pumped out 'Rock Around the Clock'

One night, when collecting some bathing gear from the back yard, I found a huddle of guests standing transfixed. In the light streaming from Rosemarie's open chalet door she could be seen dancing with abandon oblivious to her audience, dark curls flying and eyes blazing, she looked like some pagan Nereid. As she circled stamping fiercely with her outstretched hands brandishing a mop, she crooned in a deep haunting voice, 'I dance, I dance, I lof you,' and she kissed the mop. 'I 'ate you' and she hurled it to the ground. 'I weel keel you.' Then throwing arms wide stamped on the handle, 'I joomp on your estomach' and she threw herself prostrate across the mop!

Awed we crept silently away. Here was some teenage rite, which defied analysis. We felt it was small wonder that Rosemarie's mother was anxious.

She caused quite a sensation when she fell violently in love with one of the guests. He and companion had turned up unexpectedly, like two birds of paradise. He was the choreographer from the Windmill, Piccadilly and had arrived with an exotic young male companion. Both walking gracefully on neat arched feet they swayed into the dining room bringing all conversation to an abrupt standstill.

I never discovered how they had heard of The Seagull, but there they were glamorously outlandish, tanned to a crisp, clad in brilliantly eccentric garments, not at all in keeping with our more sober guests.

Rosemarie fell ardently in love with the choreographer and as token of this passion and perhaps to enliven the dullness of bed making, she took to laying red roses (mine) on his pillow. Elsie did not approve, but like all of us was swept along by Rosemarie's forceful character. Shaking with indignation she complained to me.

'I shouldn't worry too much Elsie' I consoled. 'He looks well able to cope. He must have met this kind of adoration often.'

'Huumph,' she grunted 'I shouldn't wonder, but this isn't the right place for such goings on.'

Despite my warning that it was all wasted effort Rosemarie persevered, enthusiastically extending her passion to the dining room by laying a red rose (mine again) on his table napkin. His friend took umbrage and a tetchy muted argument ensued, rising to a hysterical outburst with Francesca fluttering anxiously between them.

Throwing the offending rose to the floor the friend flounced out, feet neatly placed, hips swinging even more elegantly, leaving a room full of fascinated onlookers who had watched this unfolding drama with morbid curiosity for the past few days.

For many years Nick was the undisputed ruler of the back yard where he lived out his vivid fantasies. Twelve foot walls gave him his first taste of danger; chasing rats his first hunting adventures, electrical experiments his first scientific experience, sending everyone hysterical as taps emitted shocks and sparks instead of water.

Airguns popped at astounded pigeons, arrows whizzed by astonished pantry maids and for years the yard echoed with the excited cries of small boys' breathless battles.

But all was not play, Nick, like the rest, had his work to do. From the age of twelve he was responsible for peeling the potatoes. Each morning seven or eight buckets full had to be fed into the electric peeler. and then laboriously 'eyed'. To make a dull job more entertaining he devised a complex pulley-system; endangering all lives, as buckets slopping water whirled at top speed from pantry to peeler, thence to kitchen while back-firing potatoes in its unsteady wake.

Our system may not have been entirely orthodox, but the work got done with the minimum amount of grumbles and the maximum amount of fun. It may not have been accomplished in the most professional way, yet from the guest's point of view it appeared to give that effect, judging by their comments and The Seagull's growing popularity.

CHAPTER 21

1952/3 – THE GASTRONOMES

Gradually The Seagull's success was assured. A local gastronomic club made us their centre. A Wine and Food Society included us in their South Western circuit. We made many new friends, lost few old ones. The permanent staff settled down, augmented each Spring by a string of lively young European students.

My bank manager, Mr.Canny was all smiles these days, apart from his winter depression which enveloped him like a pea-soup for the first five months of every year. He was unable or unwilling to remember that by June the winter's overdraft would be wiped out, that by August I should be able to reduce the loan by £1000 or more. Temperamental as an adolescent his spirits rose and fell with predictable regularity.

It was early September in 1952 when I bounced into his office sure of a welcome and the small glass of sherry which greeted me from June onwards and which abruptly ceased in January.

'I want to borrow £3,000' I said optimistically after the usual courtesies had been exchanged. Mr. Canny's face fell into its customary cautious gloom.

'Good gracious Mrs. Richards, you can't be serious. Why you've only just reduced your winter overdraft.'

'Yes – by £750 I chipped in. We've had a very good season now I want to expand.' I beamed at him encouragingly.

Mr. Canny wasn't going to be hustled, looking at me severely over his spectacles he answered grudgingly 'Yes, you have a nice little business down there, if you keep on as you're going you should be clear of debt in less than three years. I see you have nearly paid off the second mortgage to Mr. Barclay. Very satisfactory – very satisfactory indeed but we mustn't rush into another large debt must we?' I could feel his palm itching to pat the little woman's head.

'I know,' I replied politely, longing to add – not thanks to any encouragement from you and that dreary head office.

'That's exactly why I want to borrow a further £3,000. Let me explain,' I gulped down my sherry in order to give myself courage.

'As you know we are getting well known for our good food but its an awful handicap not having a licence. People have to bring their wine with them so the profit goes elsewhere. The residents keep bottles up in their bedrooms in a secretive way and we are always having to send one of the staff dashing out for drinks when we can least spare them. The whole thing is a terrible waste of time and energy.' I stopped for breath. I did not add that the busy staff more often than not hustled only as far as my office, where I kept an illicit supply!

Mr. Canny queried guardedly. 'Why should getting a licence necessitate borrowing £3,000?'

'Well, if we get a table licence and I'm almost sure I can get one, we will have to have a room where people can gather to drink in comfort. As you know the basement is almost all useless space. Apart from the playroom the guests use none of it, neither is it really suitable as staff quarters. Now, if we converted the whole of that area into a new dining room, kitchens, pantry, and store-rooms, also a decent men's cloakroom which we badly need, the present dining room on the first floor would become the new sitting room. The kitchen could be a cocktail lounge and I'd convert the sitting room into two new double bedrooms both overlooking the sea. With the extra money I would make from these two rooms, without even thinking about the extra profit from a new and bigger dining room and the profit on drinks, I could soon pay back the £3,000.'

Mr. Canny glinted at me cautiously, nodding his bald head as he scribbled down a few figures, I could see he was becoming interested.

'But what would all these alterations cost? What about all those students you take on – where would you put them?'

'I'd convert some more of the outhouses into little chalets – no problem there. I've gone into costs very carefully with a reliable builder. He is pretty sure the whole job could be done for £2,500. That would leave me £500 to buy carpets, curtains and new furniture.'

'Yes, yes,' he murmured judiciously writing down a few more figures. 'I suppose I could put the suggestion to Head Office. I know they are very pleased with how you've managed so far Mrs. Richards but it's a lot of money on top of your remaining debt, which stands at – let me see,' he rang for the balance sheet. After studying it carefully he added, 'a little over £2,500.'

I could see I should lose ground if I let him dwell on this theme for too long, so bade him a swift goodbye before he could think up any more depressing reasons why a loan should not be forthcoming.

To Mr. Canny's surprise Head Office gave their approval and just after Christmas The Seagull once more became a jungle of whistling plasterers, bricklayers, painters and carpenters. Gradually out of the useless dismal dark basement emerged an enchanting L-shaped dining room in gleaming ivory, deep coral and the softest of hydrangea blues. A specially carved oak door led into a newly constructed cellar (formerly the scene of the mad lovelorn commando's night escapades) housing our now legal wines. The old central heating boiler was ripped out of the playroom and the gaping hole was converted into a deep curved alcove which, subtly lit, made a perfect setting for the choicest pieces of my almost priceless collection of Royal Copenhagen china, which we used for special dinner parties. A large pantry led out of the dining room, its jade green-tiled floor gleaming through the two swing doors.

Beyond this lay the kitchen where Cookie grumbled her way round the newly installed Aga. 'I'll never get used to this. She'll never work down here -will you dear?' giving it an affectionate pat.

'I'm sure the chimney is all the wrong way. Fancy having a kitchen facing this way! Now where has that dratted boy put the charcoal?' she muttered as she twisted the nine newspaper coils which are superstitiously reputed to be necessary to get Agas alight. But gradually, grudgingly she had to admit that the new kitchen was far superior to the old one; entailed far less walking about for her poor feet; and involved her in fewer visits from chatty guests who now rarely penetrated through the protective swing doors.

The renovations were carried out in the spring of 1953 by a Mr. Priaux, a man of integrity, who completed the work in three months keeping exactly to his estimate of £2,500. As before, once the foreman had faded out of the scene and I had direct contact, the men responded to praise and were as eager as I to finish the job by Easter. We never did discover what happened to Jacksy. He simply disappeared after a week of acrimoniously lengthy discussions between himself and Mr. Priaux while the men stood moodily around – 'browned off' and inactive.

After that unproductive week we found we were all on good terms. If I found the chaps sitting around doing nothing, I'd ask why, only to be told, 'The bricks haven't arrived Mum.' An immediate phone call, using guile, persuasion or even 'helpless little woman' tactics produced the bricks within hours.

'We can't get on with the painting,' moaned the painters. 'They've sent the wrong colour.'

'Come on help me with it into the car, I'll go and fetch it,' and off I'd go with gallons of bright green paint instead of the ivory we'd ordered.

Mr. Priaux protested mildly at first, hinting in his gentle way, 'We'll have trouble if you interfere too much.'

To this I briskly replied, 'Let's deal with that when it occurs. They seem happy enough at the moment. Better still they have a sense of urgency and that suits all of us.' Then I added rashly, 'The sooner women are enrolled as foremen the better, don't you agree?'

Mr. Priaux nodding sadly left us to manage in our own unorthodox fashion!

By sealing the top of the back stairs with thick boarding the dirt and noise was kept to the minimum. Surprisingly I received none of the complaints I'd been anticipating from our few winter residents.

We opened the new dining room with a party, the first I had given since coming to Exmouth six years ago. Choosing the week before the Easter holiday, 250 invitations were issued.

After giving the few residents a swift breakfast we settled down to prepare a magnificent smörgesbrod; 160 French loaves sliced and buttered; 60 different delicious spreads prepared, lobster, crab, chicken caviar, smoked salmon, fresh salmon, smoked trout, smoked eel, pate, prawns and turkey. The choice was endless. 20 different cheeses nestled on pumpernickel and whole meal bread. Cookie poured her soul into making chocolate eclairs, rhum babas, hazelnut meringues, fruit flans, lemon meringue pies and many more sweets.

Nick and Lu gathered branches of apple and pear blossom and bunches of wild flowers. Candelabras gleamed with candles alight and the new dining room sparkled a dazzling welcome. The wine cellar, manned by Frank and his six brothers, held two giant kegs of wine. It was a joyous christening for phase three of The Seagull's history.

CHAPTER 22

1954 – KIDDIE'S MEALS OR HAUTE CUISINE?

It is a doubtful blessing for a small family hotel to gain a reputation for good food. The two ought to go together. It sounds simple enough as it works well in the rest of Europe, but in Britain the problems it presents are endless.

Take breakfast, an awkward meal at the best of times, one which seekers after gastronomic gems will probably eschew altogether, being no doubt tucked up in bed recovering from the delicacies of the night before. But one cannot bank on this. The gastronome is, if in a hotel famed for its food, just as likely to expect a choice of freshly grilled trout, devilled kidneys or kedgeree along with an array of egg dishes. To produce breakfast for fifty people of varying ages, including infants who require boiled milk and 'just a lightly coddled egg if you please', requires the concentrated skill of a well trained team, especially if the toast is to be crisp, the coffee hot and the bacon done to a turn.

In our case, because we charged rates that the over burdened family man could afford, staff were kept to a minimum. But apart from this, anyone who has catered for children knows that to offer the simplest choice invites disaster.

Friends sometimes found these facts hard to assimilate. Dinah and Jack were typical. They wanted to stay at The Seagull because of the warmth of welcome and the good food, knowing that their three children enjoyed its relaxed atmosphere. But they were wealthy and well able to afford more luxurious surroundings. They therefore made not so veiled comparisons which I found aggravating.

One spring Jack rang from a hotel on the other side of the county. 'Kirstine come over and dine with us tonight. We're staying at a lovely place, I'm sure you would enjoy their cooking.' So off I went. It was a lovely place situated at the end of a long drive, perched on the edge of an exquisite forest overlooking the sea. The menu was imposing with a choice of six delicious sounding dishes including Lobster Thermidor, Chestnut Stuffed Pheasant (odd this in late April) Oyster Pie and Frogs Legs.

I noticed that the main menu; a simple one, presented no choice at all, just melon, soup, roast and desert. The other dishes were priced as extras ranging from twenty seven pounds and sixpence upwards.

After due consideration we each ordered something different. As there were six of us I felt it was an expensive way of teaching me a lesson.

We waited. My trained eye could see there was a crisis behind the scenes. The two waitresses looked close to tears, and guests were becoming restive. In just over an hour our chosen dishes arrived. They were good but the wine which Jack had ordered when we sat down arrived with the sweet, so had to be corked up again for another day. Francesca would have been appalled.

Whilst we were having coffee mine host arrived looking distraught, at once plunging into the sort of conversation dear to the heart of all hoteliers, entailing the difficulties and frustrations of running a hotel.

'It's terrible,' he moaned. 'This is only our second season and the fourteenth chef left this morning. My wife is at the end of her tether as she has to fill the gap every time. She anyway has to do most of the cooking as these chefs don't seem up to the job and always need help.'

I made sympathetic noises staring at Jack who looked bland.

'I noticed you have a pretty long menu for such a small place,' I murmured. 'I'd find it difficult to produce all seven dishes perfectly cooked at such varied times,' for I had noticed outside guests were still arriving as we left the dining room.

'Well of course,' he answered, 'our prices are high to enable us to employ at least three chefs. but it's difficult to get them to come out here. When we have the full complement they quarrel among themselves or grumble at the amount of work or the distance we are from Bideford. I lay on a car to take them to and fro but they still complain, then leave at a moment's notice, so it all comes back upon my poor wife. It's killing her.'

Here he dropped his voice to a whisper. 'I've put the place up for sale. We can't wait to get out.'

Hoping Jack and Dinah were taking this in I asked innocently, 'How much do you charge?'

'Twenty four guineas a week out of season, then from the middle of July to the end of September, thirty five guineas.'

Thinking of our pathetic eight guineas rising to twelve in the height of the season, I asked, 'Do you make any reduction for children?'

He looked shocked. 'Most certainly not. They occupy the same space as adults, usually eat more and do more damage. No, no we charge full rates for all children.'

He looked severely at Jack's three children rollicking about on his elegant chairs.

I hoped my friends got the full implication of this conversation, but doubted it as their children still moaned over our limited choice, when next they stayed at The Seagull.

Conversations like the following had soon changed our early ambition of serving a varied breakfast menu.

'Darling what will you have this morning?' Fond mother anxiously looking at son whilst our waiter, Leslie. hopped impatiently from foot to foot.

'A boiled egg.'

'But sweetheart it's a long time till lunch. Don't you think you should have some bacon, perhaps a sausage?'

'1 want an egg.'

'What do you think dearest?' turning to father deep in his paper. 'Don't you think Peter ought to have more than an egg?' 'What, what? What was that? Oh let the boy have what he wants.'

'All right then Leslie, lightly boiled for just three and a half minutes,' says the still doubtful mother.

'Now pet,' turning to daughter 'What will you have?'

'Daddy what are you going to have?'

'Who me? Well what is there? Now let me see. How about some mushrooms, bacon, perhaps two fried eggs, eh Leslie?' shooting him a 'man to man' glance with a hint of a tip in his eye.

'I'll have the same mummy.'

'But pet, you don't like mushrooms, they always upset you.'

'I do today and they don't,' says daughter Pet looking tearful.

'All right then Leslie' mother mutters hastily.

'I'll have, now let me think, perhaps a poached egg on toast, no on fried bread.'

Leslie goes off thankfully to give the order only to meet Peter's head poking through the hatch several minutes later, 'I've changed my mind. I'll have a kipper instead.'

After several weeks of this with breakfast ending around eleven o'clock, our staff's nerves in shreds, we decided to serve a different breakfast each day, with no choice. This was practical but hardly qualified us for the top gastronomic stakes nor for unwary diners clutching 'The Good Food Guide' or 'Let's Halt Awhile'. For those food connoisseurs it was a nasty enough shock to be confronted by an array of lively toddlers, highchairs, buckets and spades, without a strictly limited menu as well, however well cooked.

Balanced on this tightrope, I gradually trained our diners to order specialities well in advance. Anyone unwary or ignorant enough to brave The Seagull at lunch time had to take pot luck and a mob of children munching their way through the 'dish of the day'. By evening the place was swept clear of all young by the simple expedient of laying on a generous buffet supper at 6.00pm and charging full rates for any child sitting up to dinner. Magically the dining room became civilised with candles, wine, well behaved teenagers and not a toddler in sight.

I knew The Seagull had arrived, gastronomically speaking, when on one of Clifford's fleeting visits he said, 'Come on put on your bonnet. I'll take you out for the day, give you a slap up dinner, one that you haven't had to brood over yourself.'

We had a gorgeous day. Somewhere in the middle of Dartmoor we stopped for a drink.

'Tell me' said Clifford to mine host, 'Tell me where we can go for a really good meal.'

'Ah Sir, there's only one place in these parts that I can thoroughly recommend, but that's a long way from here. The Seagull in Exmouth is the place for you, but that's all of thirty miles from here and I'm told you have to book days in advance.'

He looked amazed when we burst out laughing. I didn't know whether to be gratified or sad that good dinners were so rare in the South West.

When a local wine connoisseur, John Sutton, made us the centre for his exclusive gastronomic feasts, we suddenly found ourselves embarrassingly popular and our trouble really started.

The day the Archbishop of Canterbury came to lunch was not one of our gastronomic triumphs. On a dreary Monday in early January knowing I had Nick's school trunk to pack I planned a simple meal for the handful of residents, well within Margaret's capabilities.

Margaret, who had started her career as kitchen maid in a grand house in Belgravia, was an excellent plain cook. She came to The Seagull as pantry maid but after Cookie left to start her own small guest house, became my assistant, handling straight-forward roasts and stews most efficiently.

I heard the gong and glancing at the clock thought, 'Excellent, bang on one o'clock. Margaret is a gem.' Suddenly the door of Nick's chalet flew open. Francesca burst in.

'Come quick boss – the Archbishop of Canterbury is here. You must come!'

'Six, seven eight,' I muttered, 'why do schools want so much of everything? Francesca, if the Queen herself were here I could do nothing about it. You must cope.' I went on counting socks.

'But,' began Francesca, then seeing my fierce concentration heaved a sigh and dashed off muttering German lamentations.

Several minutes later her dramatic announcement penetrated my brain. Through a haze of vests and pyjamas I rose reluctantly. What a day for an Archbishop to choose and why Exmouth? I suppose I'll have to go and ask him if he's enjoying his lunch. Then with a nasty jolt I realized just what an unimaginative meal he must have been offered. I hadn't the nerve to face his 'august presence' over Irish Stew and Apple Dumplings so my only memory of the Archbishop was seeing him speeding through the hall, plump with dumplings, eager to bless the new stained glass window commemorating Churchill in Trinity Church.

We were not always so unprepared as on that occasion. I could usually face guests feeling proud of our efforts even though some were achieved with difficulty. Whilst Cookie was still with me she rarely penetrated far from her kitchen, but one morning she appeared with turban askew in a state of even more agitation than usual.

'Kirstine I'm not having wild animals let loose in my kitchen. You must do something. They're stamping around like elephants.'

'What are?' I snarled looking up from a column of figures. 'I'll be down directly. Shut the door when you go out. Beetles I suppose, or mice what a fuss.'

'No Kirstine, you must come now. Cray fish, great big horrible cray fish are tramping round my kitchen.'

'Oh those' I exclaimed. 'Splendid, John Sutton promised we'd have them in good time.'

'Well I'm not going in there again until you've dealt with them. It's one thing to cook fancy dinners, but quite another to have to hunt and kill your quarry first.'

Cookie stalked off enraged.

Peels of merriment greeted me as I descended the stairs a huddle of excited students greeting me with cries of, 'Watch out boss – don't go in there.'

'Rubbish!' I snorted, marching into the kitchen. Just as quickly backing out, slamming the door behind me. Two enormous crayfish like prehistoric handbags were rattling their way in my direction.

'Gosh' I though. 'However are we supposed to get those in a pot – and which pot?' The recipe for 'Crayfish a la Normandy' read laconically, 'Drop live crayfish in a pot of boiling wine.' How much wine for those two I wondered – a barrel at least. I called Nick and his cousin Tim.

'Would you each like to earn five shillings?'

'Rather' was the swift reply.

'Well you two are the crayfish keepers for today. It's your job to help us when it comes to cooking the brutes tonight.'

The next twenty minutes were spent in fielding the enraged animals into the boiler house where, tied with stout rope, they could be heard for the rest of the day scraping angrily amidst the ashes which hardly seemed a good gastronomic prelude. That evening with the 'consommé celestine' simmering gently, Cookie and I prepared the largest preserving pan we possessed, then standing well back watched the boys as they staggered in with their infuriated burdens. Covering our ears to drown the squeals, we watched with horror as the poor creatures endeavoured to escape from the bubbling brew. Never again we vowed, would we follow a recipe which started, 'Take a live crustacean – place it in boiling wine...' I have since learned that shellfish are far more tender if placed in cold liquid and allowed to die gently as the heat rises.

Not all our gastronomic dinners were so traumatic but few were entirely without incident. The very first was one of these. Cookie and I, quivering nervously like greyhounds, had planned what we considered a memorable meal. John Sutton had given days of concentrated consideration and innumerable telephone calls about the choice of suitable wines. Alan Sichel, from Bordeaux, world famous wine exporter, was to be the guest of honour.

Seven portly gentlemen, resplendent in dinner jackets and boiled shirts, foregathered in my sitting room titillating their gastric juices with sips of iced champagne in front of a crackling log fire. I was tasting the 'consommé aux oeuf' reflectively when June, the young trainee, appeared looking anxious.

'There's a policeman in the hall in a flap about a parked car in the neighbours driveway. He says it's got to be moved.'

'Oh' I was abstracted. 'Tell him it can't be one of ours.' Then I remembered the gastronomes, adding, 'I suppose it could be one of theirs. Go and ask Mr. Sutton, June.'

'I've done that' she answered, 'It's Dr. Geidt's. He just laughed, said it wasn't hurting anyone. He's in one of his puckish moods.' She shot me a knowing look.

Bother the man I thought. I knew David when the devil got into him, stubborn as a two year old and mischievous as any teenager.

'Ask Francesca to get him to shift it. He'll do anything for her, but DONT BOTHER ME!'

I returned to the soup. Several minutes later Francesca dashed in looking flustered.

'Zey are all ready now. Can we start serving ze zoup? I can't get ze docteur to do anyzing but geegle. Zey aff six more vines to go. I zink ees a leetly squeefed already' she raised her eyebrows eloquently. She and June disappeared with the soup tureen.

'That policeman is still there,' said June when collecting the 'Tout de Paris' a delicious melange of sole, shrimps, lobster, asparagus, almonds and grapes nestling cosily in a luscious white wine sauce. 'He's absolutely furious. He insists on seeing you.'

'Tell him I can do nothing now. As soon as we've dished up

the next course I'll come and move the wretched thing myself, but tell him this is a most important occasion. I must deal with the dinner first.'

June was back in a few minutes almost in tears. 'He won't go. Francesca is busy pouring wines. I think he's going to arrest me – he's absolutely livid.' She grabbed the pomme d'eclair.

'Look June tell him to go into the dining room. If he wants to arrest anyone he'll have to arrest Dr. Geidt himself. It's his problem, not mine.' I turned to help Cookie dish up the Cotelette de Veau à la Maintenon.

A silence fell in the dining room as the seven diners bent their heads low over their plates, wilfully ignoring the embarrassed policeman who stood uncertain in the doorway. Angry but awed by the splendid array of boiled shirts, he hesitated, then clearing his throat nervously boomed.

'Gentlemen, I mean Sirs. In the name of the law I authorize you to remove the car which is parked on private... ' his voice petered out, a look of horror wiping out the angry expression on his face. Tentatively he removed his helmet then remembering his position, put it on again. His eyes were rivetted, not on Dr. Geidt, whom he knew well as the police surgeon, but on a handsome middle aged man seated facing him. No one had warned the poor chap that he would come face to face with the Chief Constable of the County. The silence was broken by a roar of laughter.

'Do your duty man,' shouted the Chief Constable.

'Arrest that man,' roared John Sutton.

'Mon Dieu – quel horreur!' cried Monsieur Sichel.

'Gross Gott!' exclaimed Francesca pouring the Chateau Cos D'istournel St. Estephe 1929 all over the table.

There was a mouselike squeak from June as the poor policeman shrank into his size thirteen boots. Then manfully he rallied, finished his sentence and David Geidt, rocking with mirth, went to shift his car.

In two minutes he was back.

'I don't move that car until the people who have scribbled all over it clean it up. They've broken the law by defacing my car.' He sat down.

The wretched bobby, having by now quite lost track of what was legal and what was not, miserably tramped off. A few minutes later to the delight of the seven diners the owners of the hotel next door could be seen earnestly scrubbing away under the stern eyes of the law. Only when his car was reported clean by the chastened policeman did David shift his car, giggling wickedly all the while.

The dinner was pronounced a high success and Monsieur Sichel returned to France more convinced than ever of the eccentricity of the British.

On another occasion Cookie greeted me ominously, 'Those pheasants aren't going to do.'

'What do you mean – not do?' Of course they'll do. Four pheasants for seven people with all the trimmings that should be plenty.'

'I don't mean that,' she answered tetchily staring at the four birds lying on the kitchen table.

'I mean they're not 'high' enough. You know how fussy John Sutton is. These birds don't smell I don't think they've been hung at all.' She sniffed at them suspiciously.

They certainly didn't smell of anything much except raw flesh and stale feathers. We gazed at them appalled, for John viewed such culinary lapses gravely. What could we do? There must be something that hurried along the process of decomposition, but what? It was maddening because I knew all explanation of my long careful discussions with the supplier would be brushed aside. As far as John was concerned, we had slipped up, his dinner would be ruined. Six hours to go, those birds just had to be good and 'high' – but how?

'You must do something' cried my sister as she always did in moments of crisis.

'I can't stop now, I'm all behind.' She bustled off to chivvy the baker who was standing patiently riveted to this drama, no doubt eager to spread the story all round Exmouth.

As all good cooks with initiative know, the solution lay at my elbow. The pheasants were duly roasted and the diners expressed their pleasure.

'Those birds were done to a turn. Never,' they cried 'never had pheasants tasted so perfect. How long had they been hung, where, at what temperature?'

I did not feel it was seemly to tell them how carefully Cookie and I had rubbed the birds, both inside and out with Italy's best gorgonzola, but I felt it was a pity that true genius had to pass unnoticed.

I was often asked why I had never remarried.

'There's never any time for courting,' was my stock reply.

'Well what do you do exactly?' one friend persevered.

After deep thought all I could honestly say was, 'I put the parsley on.'

CHAPTER 23

ON THE WAVE OF CULINARY SUCCESS

Over the years we became well known for good food largely through the recommendation of food writers such as Andre Simon[2], Raymond Postgate[3] and Ashley Courtenay[4]. Our reputation was enhanced, oddly enough, through a Fanny Craddock article although it was mainly through the gastronomes who sometimes entertained visiting wine specialists of the calibre of the Bordeaux Sichels.

Our reputation was made, not because of enormous menus offering all manner of frozen dishes hastily slapped under hot grills, but because my sister and I had inherited from our Danish father his insistence on the best quality fish or meat being cooked with pure butter, fresh cream and farm eggs. No synthetics were allowed to enter our kitchen and for that matter, after our first unhappy experience with Leslie, no hotel trained chefs either.

A love of French travel, sensitive palates and the spirit of adventure had completed our culinary training.

[2] Andre Simon (28th February 1877 – 5th September 1970) was a French born wine merchant, gourmet and prolific wine writer. Hugh Johnson describes him as "the charismatic leader of the English wine trade for almost all of the first half of the 20th century, and the grand old man of literate connoisseurship for a further twenty years".

[3] Raymond William Postgate (6th November 1896 – 29th march 1971) was an English socialist, author, journalist and editor, social historian, mystery novelist and gourmet, who founded the Good Food Guide.

[4] Ashley Courtenay's hotel guide Let's Halt Awhile1947 and other publications.

Owing to pressure from some of our regular visitors who felt we ought to be included in The A A Guide Book, I wrote to ask if we could be visited by one of their Inspectors. I then put the matter out of my head.

A few weeks later in early Spring a tall elderly gentleman asked for a room for the night. I settled him comfortably then returned to the kitchen where we were preparing, as I thought, a particularly appetising meal for the resident guests. Although we served a limited choice of main dishes, we made the provision for visitors wishing to have special dinners to order them in advance.

'Who is the newcomer?' said the invaluable Francesca, so caring that no guest left our dining room without a feeling of well-being.

'He's peering at ze menu most suspiciously – doesn't seem to like anyzing.'

'Never mind' I was smug. 'Wait until he tastes the almond cream soup. One sip of that and he'll relax you'll see. I don't think we've ever made one that tastes nicer.'

Almond soup was one of our specialities greatly praised by knowing guests.

'Vell,' said Francesca, 'He's eating but doesn't look as zough he's enjoying it very much but he's chosen the veal olives so he's certain to enjoy zat. Everyone has gone mad about zem, zey all want ze recipe.'

A pity, I thought. I would have liked him to try the kidneys and mushrooms sautéed in sherry and cream, they taste particularly good tonight, or lobster with our home-made mayonnaise and potato salad fragrant with herbs, the lobsters so fresh that I had difficulty in cracking and cooling them in time for dinner. They looked marvellously appetising sitting in their green nests of crisp lettuce.

'He is peculiar' Francesca told me. 'I asked heem if he had enjoyed the veal olives. He vas most surprised and grudgingly admitted, 'I didn't expect to but they were eatable!' Now he is wondering whether to have the peppermint ice cream or the hazelnut meringue pudding.'

She came out a few moments later look disappointed 'He's just told me zat he's never heard of peppermint ice cream and can't eat nuts!'

'I told him the ice cream was one of our specialities, that it's coated in hot chocolate wiz whipped cream, but he looked unhappy, so could you knock up a leetle lemon pancake? Zat might cheer him up. Perhaps he'll enjoy the cheese.'

She whisked off determined to please this difficult guest.

We were very proud of our cheeses – never less than eight and nine different kinds, always served at the correct degree of maturity. But he refused the cheese board leaving the dining room exuding displeasure.

The next morning Mr. X. introduced himself as the Inspector from the AA. I waited confidently, so used to the paean of praise from departing guests, that even if he hadn't shown much pleasure over his dinner he must have appreciated the comfort of his bedroom, the boiling hot water, or the charm of my attentive young staff in their pretty hand-embroidered lacy aprons.

He looked gloomy as he paid his bill saying lugubriously,

'Of course I can't possibly recommend this hotel to the Association; it doesn't rate one star. I wouldn't feel safe in suggesting that it should even be mentioned in our guide book.'

Astounded I gasped, 'In heaven's name why not?'

Looking even more morose he rasped, 'The food, we couldn't possibly accept the standard of your food.'

'What do you mean? Everyone's raving about it. You must have heard them yourself?' For this particular group of guests were even more appreciative than most.

'I cooked your dinner myself. I know it was delicious.'

'Yes, that's true, I heard all those people sending messages out to the cook. They may well have liked it but,' he drew himself up proudly, 'Our clientele wouldn't like it at all. Why, you didn't have a roast joint on the menu. Everyone wants a roast after a journey.'

He paused then added querulously, 'Who ever heard of almond cream soup and what about those puddings. I've never heard of either of them. Now a vanilla or strawberry ice cream, that would have been the ticket, that's what our people want, or a jam sponge with custard. We'd never get away with hazelnut meringue pudding or peppermint ice cream, not with our people' He gazed at me indignantly.

'What about the lovely choice of cheese?' I demanded.

'Cheese – cheese – I don't eat cheese. Anyway I've got a duodenal ulcer. That meat dish you gave me didn't sit at all comfortably.'

'What about the beautiful dining room, surely you must admit that must count for something. Most of the AA places I've been to all look exactly the same all serving the same horribly dull food.'

By now I was very angry. 'We do have roasts often, but usually have them at lunch time. We try to make the evening meals more interesting.'

'That may well be, but this would never do for our people.' Then he added, 'I was coming to the dining room. Where were the table cloths? Did your girls forget to put them on? Nice white table cloths is what we like to see.'

'But we always have polished tables,' I spluttered. 'White table cloths make every dining room look identical. Our rosewood and walnut tables are lovely with candles and flowers.'

I could have hit him he was so stupid, so sure of the rightness of his dreary opinion.

'And,' here he paused dramatically, 'that bedroom you gave me, the bed didn't have a headboard. You can't give people beds with no headboard.'

'Of course you can,' I nearly added 'You silly man. They are divans and don't need headboards.' I was thinking wryly of the struggle we'd had in finding beds and our joy when we found those magical divans.

'Oh, our people would want headboards,' he answered pompously. 'Why, we'd have thousands of complaints a year from people up and down the country. Everyone wants head boards. But I'll tell you this,' he looked judicial, 'There is one good thing about this hotel, your gentlemen's cloakroom is very nice, very nice indeed.' With that he buttoned his overcoat and left. I never heard anything from the AA and it didn't make a whit of difference to our success.

Much later in the year on a dismal afternoon I found a small angry man standing at the front door.

'I'm the labour inspector I want to examine your labour relationships.'

I was amazed. I never knew there were such things, but invited him in offering him tea, hoping to soften his resentful attitude.

'No thank you, I want to interview your staff.'

He looked even more irritated and suspicious when I told him there was no one around who could be interviewed, it being 3.00 pm in the Winter season. All but one were off-duty and that one had slipped out to the shops ten minutes ago.

'You must have someone on duty. You're open aren't you?' he asked belligerently.

'Yes we are but I am here to deal with guests. However, June will be back shortly to do the afternoon tea. You can talk to her.

'She will be a good candidate as she's been with us for two years. There's nothing she doesn't know about The Seagull's methods.'

I tried to question him about his work but he was guarded. He simply told me that he covered the West Country from Bristol to Lands End. He obviously didn't much like what he saw. Luckily June came in soon. I left them alone whilst dealing with the teas. When I took theirs in, he was firing questions at a bewildered June, but being a co-operative girl she was valiantly dealing with this grilling.

After two hours the inspector sent her to say he'd like to talk to me.

'Mrs. Richards I am more than satisfied,' he began. 'I have covered every aspect of the work pattern here and I can find nothing to criticise. May I say this is most unusual. In fact, since I started this job several years ago I have been appalled. Your hotel is the only, I repeat this, the only hotel where the staff are not exploited one way or the other. Either their wages are fiddled or they work hours that are too long. You've no idea how employers manipulate the Wages and Catering Act'.

'Now, your staff work a forty hour week, are paid properly, even generously by other standards. You feed them well and share out the 10% service charge honestly. I assure you I have left no stone unturned in questioning your girl. (I could believe that). I congratulate you.' He almost smiled as he marched out of the door.

June still looking bemused told me he'd penetrated into every corner of her life, even where she hung her smalls to dry. We giggled a bit as we marvelled at this sudden appearance of a representative of a department of which we'd known nothing.

I am sure he would have been surprised to know he had introduced a note of unexpected glamour into a very boring November day.

Chapter 24

A Search for the Right Man!

Now that The Seagull was well established, restlessness set in as I had more time to look around. It had always been painful for me to see fathers with their children for it made it very clear how much my own two were missing. A father to brag about, to emulate and to adore. Whichever way you tackle it a family without one parent is broken backed and the effects go on from one generation to another.

I felt my children's childhood had slipped through my fingers. This knowledge hurt, that their early memories would only contain me as someone whirling around bossily absorbed in other things.

Any woman who consciously determines to have a child and bring him up on her own is sadly misguided. Her own bitter experience may have said no to marriage but she should not subject children to such a one-sided arrangement.

Apart from the psychological damage, the material disadvantages are very great. With the mother as sole wage earner big sacrifices have to be made. It is hard for children to watch their friends having treats and presents, which are denied them. Unless especially privileged, they are brought up in a restricted atmosphere and are liable to mismanage money when they begin to earn, or are unable to spend because in childhood money had been too scarce.

A working mother, unless she is blessed with excellent health, determination and self denial is almost bound to neglect her children, so they end up losing both parents. The pitfalls ahead of them, if they are cast out on their own when too young, are endless. I felt that the greatest lack had been time for gentle guidance and cherishing.

Lone mothers cannot win. If they are sturdy resourceful fighters they are in danger of sapping their children's development, if timid and hesitant their children are not encouraged sufficiently. If strong they are accused of emasculating their sons, if weak they become an intolerable burden.

I had told myself repeatedly that this life was only temporary, that when the struggle was over I would return to normality and become a docile loving woman. But now I wondered. Piracy had been fun. Pitting one's wits against bureaucracy is fun. Making decisions, skillfully manoeuvering difficult people or awkward situations and being the boss is all fun. I had tried to convince myself that this toughness was necessary simply in order to survive, but I knew in my heart that I enjoyed the heady satisfaction of being my own boss; of wriggling around the rules; of defying the stupidity of much that hampers freedom of action.

If I married, I mused guiltily, I'd be able to give the children a more stable background. I pictured a passive cozy mother in a neat cozy house with time to listen to their problems and time to give them the emotional support they so obviously needed now they had reached adolescence. But would I be able to fit into this calm oasis after my exciting frenzied nerve-wracking life with its achievements, anxieties, despairs and heady satisfactions?

It also crossed my mind that there would have to be a neat cozy husband to fit into this fantasy. Though no beauty, I'd never lacked admirers and at forty two considered that it was not too late to embark on romance. If I smartened up a bit, used my spare time more intelligently, studied other women's techniques more assiduously maybe I could get back into the romantic swim. Time enough then to see how we all fitted into this idyllic dream.

None of this thinking was clear cut, simply a muddled and anguished ache for something that was missing.

It was at this point that a large bombastic chief of police zoomed into my life. Recently divorced and on leave from some distant African outpost, with the custody of his two small daughters (although they were not in evidence) he was seeking a wife. He courted me with zest. When his leave was over we parted on ambiguous though affectionate terms. In the following months his letters became increasingly passionate, with at last the question would I marry him during his next leave?

It seemed to my cautious mind a tenuous proposition. We had danced and played lightheartedly but he knew nothing of the real me and I suspected cared less. I didn't know his children and he'd hardly noticed mine. I didn't know Africa and knew nothing of a policeman's lot. It would mean giving up a life I enjoyed – for what?

Security – perhaps? A shoulder to weep on? Somehow I didn't see him as very sympathetic to weeping women. The love of a good man? Maybe, although 'goodness' hadn't been Henry's most outstanding characteristic in those turbulent few weeks. It was more an airy bland of self satisfaction with a loud voice attached to a jovial manner. I had no idea what lay behind all of that.

I hesitated long enough for coolness to develop. Silence ensued and the episode became submerged in the ongoing dramas of hotel life.

Months later a letter arrived. I'd be surprised to know (I wasn't) that he'd met and married a charming school teacher. They were blissfully happy and would visit on their next leave. I found myself relieved rather than dismayed, having been flattered more than romantically involved.

The following spring there on my doorstep stood the jovial policeman flanked by a pale fragile blonde and two exceedingly boisterous children. They were spending their leave in a caravan at Orcombe Point.

Eying great lowering clouds surging angrily in a sullen sky I restrained a shudder as I studied the party with some misgiving. Henry was large even for a policeman, enormous for a caravan. The girls both red heads generously sprinkled with freckles, didn't look as though they would trim their energies easily to such narrow confines. The bride looked wan.

The next afternoon a tap on my door revealed the young wife, distraught and hysterical.

'C... c... could I have a b... bath' she whimpered through an avalanche of tears.

One look told me that a double gin was needed more than a bath.

'It's all s... so awful' she moaned later, as we sat eating hot buttered toast in front of a blazing fire, the wind howling mournfully in the chimney and waves crashing on the shingle.

'I'm s... so m... miserable... it's so c... cold on that h . horrible cliff. He's s... so big... so noisy and the ch... children,' here she broke off sniffing piteously.

'The ch... children... they are monsters. They do everything to m... make my life one long hell.'

I murmured something sympathetic as I put more honey on her toast.

'He goes off every morning to p... play golf leaving me to c... cope with those devils. They all eat so much and I c... can't c... cook.' Her voice rose to a wail.

'It's all quite ghastly. Why d... did I marry him? I must have been mad. He doesn't even try to understand how I f. feel... just laughs and goes off to meet his b... beastly f... friends.'

Every afternoon she arrived. Sat in a bath sipping gin and then poured out her sorrows. With smug satisfaction I thanked heaven I wasn't in her shoes.

It's a well known fact that millionaires are closely guarded by their friends and business associates lest they marry manipulative women. For some obscure reason I was once considered a suitable candidate for this exalted position.

The assessment was made discreetly by five paunchy gentlemen and my sardonic friend, Clifford, in a luxurious hotel in the middle of Dartmoor. The victim, who I am sure at that time was as innocent of their plans as I, sat abstractedly in our midst. He was fortyish, timid, plump and balding although courteously kind, if extremely nervous.

The evening passed for me in a mystified haze. Though appreciative of this unexpected bonus, an exquisite meal not cooked by me, vintage wines flowing, conversation tantalizingly just out of reach, I remained unclear as to why I was taking part in such an unlikely scenario. The stage was set, but for what? The thought flickered dreamily through my wine fuddled mind.

A few weeks later the millionaire invited me to dine in a Mayfair restaurant, so discreetly placed, that it even baffled the taxi driver. Eventually I was deposited on the correct doorstep. A dignified butler settled me in a secluded alcove in an atmosphere so subdued Westminster Abbey would have seemed riotous in comparison. A hush hung over the shadowed decor which was rich in gleaming mahogany, Persian rugs, glowing golden lamps and sad solitary diners.

Alexis arrived late, flustered and apologetic. He had been delayed by a trans-atlantic call. His nervous brown eyes under sagging lids darted anxiously in the flickering candlelight. His fingers, never still, fingered the cutlery, smoothed his few remaining tufts of hair, and plucked at the red roses which enhanced our table.

A more unlikely date was hard to imagine but millionaires had, in the fifties, the rarity value of collectors pieces. Also at that time I had a hopeful attitude towards possible suitors.

As the evening progressed even my optimism wavered as Alexis darted to and from the phone keeping in agitated touch with the vagaries of world markets, his mood swinging from wild elation to deepest despair. Not surprisingly he suffered from indigestion so whilst I tucked into luscious smoked eel, roast partridge and several delicious puddings, he swallowed handfuls of pills, his apologies as plaintive as his groans.

Between dashes to the phone he told me about his life, and my doubts about the credibility of this courtship became certainty. Despite his wealth he was as tightly trapped as any pearl in it's oyster.

He and his mother had arrived in Britain as refugees from Poland forty years earlier. They settled in a tiny flat in Kentish Town and there she intended they should remain forever. Nothing would shift her nor would she consider the smallest change in their rigid routine.

The flat was uncomfortable, inconvenient, draughty and so cramped that when Alexis changed his clothes he had to stand on his bed in order to open the wardrobe. The improvement in their financial circumstances had not budged the old lady one inch. She clung to her home as she did to her son with the tenacity of a limpet.

As the evening progressed it became increasingly clear there could be no place for me in this claustrophobic ménage. Between two strong-minded women Alexis would have been ground to a pulp. Although he knew this his eyes reflected the piteous struggle of his desperate loneliness.

As gracefully as possible I extricated myself from this abortive courtship. As we parted he touched my hand with his lips accepting a sad but inevitable farewell.

Much later I found out that my sole attribute for this assignment lay in my singular disinterest in money. I was therefore unlikely to rock the financial equilibrium of the city – a doubtful compliment.

Tony was an altogether different proposition. A practical dapper warm-hearted man in his fifties, who ran a nearby hotel and was greatly admired by his lady guests. He was a crackling spry little fellow with a fund of stories which I only half believed. He boasted of his maternal great grandmother who lived to be 116. At 108 she had pushed her 80 year old daughter across Ireland in a perambulator. He had a yellowing crinkled newspaper cutting with a faded photo of the old ladies and the pram to prove this unlikely story.

He also bragged about keeping one large double bedded room free during the season confident that holidaymakers desperate for accommodation would come thumping on his door every evening.

'I charge £5 each regardless of age or how many. If two families arrive they share the room. I've had as many as eleven in that room. That's £55 a night' he gave a chuckle, his black eyes glinting under bushy eyebrows.

'There are very few nights I don't have anyone. There's more profit in that one room than in the whole hotel. You should do the same my dear.'

Tony's greatest attribute was that he really liked women, but there was little chance of catching him between wives unless one was hyper-alert. No sooner did he return from burying one wife than he was scampering up the aisle with the next. No time for hesitation with Tony, nor courting for that matter.

He possessed an electric organ which he played loudly and with gusto in his small over full sitting room. I'm not fond of organs even in cathedrals, so even if I'd said 'snap' when the opportunity arose I somehow felt that we were not well-suited.

Willi was Norwegian, a rolicking full blooded muscular giant, whose sole possession apart from his canvases and paints appeared to be twenty six pairs of holes, rather than socks. These I industriously mended throughout one brief Brittany escapade. He appealed to me more than most, but hardly offered the placid haven I imagined we needed and would have been appalled had he known what was in my mind.

Was it fate that produced such unlikely swains or was I just fussy? Did steady reliable unattached home makers even exist or had they all been swept away by six years of war? Was I singularly inept in trying to fit the wrong pieces into the jigsaw of my life?

Could I, with more enthusiasm and speed, have made a go of it by loving Tony and his electric organ? Might I with skill have extricated Alexis from his possessive mother then distracted him from the anxieties of the stock exchange? Would I in time have learnt to love the chauvinistic policeman and his riotous red heads?

I wondered if Gerry so honourable, kind and sensitive had spoilt me for other men. I knew I could never have lived up to his high expectations but he had shown me a standard at which to aim. The children, who had inherited his qualities, I felt deserved the best. But was this just a feeble excuse because I didn't really want a settled life? Was I too proud, too fastidious, too selfish, too vain or just too damned independent?

Once I faced up to this unflattering truth I felt released, ready to start all over again, to taste without shackles all that life had to offer.

Not all The Seagull romances were so unfruitful. Brenda, the moment she set eyes on Roland, knew that this was the man for her. A young, handsome, fun loving quantity surveyor, initially elusive, he soon became a willing even eager victim. Lu, sparkling in bridesmaid taffeta escorted a radiant Brenda up the aisle. In time they had four children.

Hilde, a serious Sudentanland blonde, married Frank and his six brothers. She became a Jehovah's Witness and keeping her end up gave birth to twin boys. 'Two more' they told me proudly, 'we'll have our cricket eleven!'

Scottish Rita produced a sophisticated elegant barrister from Nigeria who when not courting perched in a corner of the kitchen languidly observing Cookie's extravaganzas with a perceptive and amused eye. At the end of the season in a flurry of good wishes, pretty Rita flew out to Lagos to marry her stylish suitor.

Cordon Bleu trained Marjorie, who worked with us briefly, was snapped up by the mischievous Dr. Geidt as his second wife.

Seductive Frances, daughter of the Lord Lieutenant of the county, conducted her flirtatious courtship with Romeo through the kitchen window. Day or night he was always there yearningly romantic. Cookie, complaining loudly, was more behind than ever that summer!

Marietta flipped off with a mysterious Latino, bringing an exquisite nut brown baby girl for our inspection the following year. I was somewhat reassured by the delay.

Our gentle baroness bewitched Scottish engineer, Neil, and they conducted their discreet courting between dining room and back yard chalet. Married in 1957 they subsequently had three children. I was proud to be god-mother to their eldest.

Courageous Joy married a lawyer, one Michael Rubenstein. They eventually had five children.

Although I didn't marry anyone, no one can say I didn't try.

CHAPTER 25

A TIME TO REFLECT

One summer evening a friend struggled into the hall looking distraught.

'I must talk to you' she said. 'I'm in terrible trouble – please help me.' She clutched at my hand for balance and to my dismay started to sob uncontrollably.

I looked round perplexed. Where would I put her? The Seagull, now in its fourteenth year, was well established, even a roaring success. The sitting room was overflowing with residents relaxing with drinks after a day on the beach. The cocktail lounge was bursting with outside parties, while my sitting room cum-office-cum-bedroom was alight with a twenty-first birthday celebration. This was no place for someone in distress but I couldn't send her away. I had to do something with her.

'Come in here' I said, steering her into the pantry past a fat man ordering a round of drinks and a thin man trying to shake my hand.

'I'll find you a chair. As soon as I can get away I'll come back and you can tell me what's troubling you.'

My mind darted anxiously to the kitchen where I ought to have been had I not been caught by one of the guests. I gave her a stiff whisky then put her crutches carefully in a corner, for Angela had the year before suffered a severe stroke becoming partially paralysed. After a hasty and I hoped comforting hug,

I dashed back to the kitchen where I was preparing several special dinners whilst also superintending the plats de jour for the resident guests.

Three hours and sixty dinners later, I remembered Angela. Filled with remorse I rushed up to the pantry but of course she'd gone.

That night I faced myself squarely and I did not like what I saw. What sort of person had I become that I could not listen to a friend in trouble because I was too busy. It sounded terrible, it was terrible to be so wound up with success and so inflated with importance.

Gloomily I reviewed the situation. Fourteen years of tremendous effort lay behind me; necessary in order to provide a livelihood for the children but was it justified now? Nick was at St. Bartholomew's Hospital, and was well on the way to becoming a doctor. Lu was immersed in her career and was dancing with the Royal Ballet. I was proud of them, being so independent and so dedicated; neither seemed to need me any longer.

When he was fourteen Nick and I had faced a major crisis. He had always found school work difficult. Report after report had said, 'Could work harder. He doesn't try, and will never pass exams'. Nick had gradually lost confidence and was settling into the role of a stupid boy. But both he and I knew that he wasn't stupid, simply uninterested. What motivates a bored child baffled both of us. Then one day in the midst of some tedious row involving wellington boots, one of which ended up in the sea, he shouted,

'I ought not to be tied to my mother's apron strings. I ought to be out exploring the world'

Exasperated I took him at his word and in a few weeks

packed him off on an Italian liner to his Uncle Guy's family in Saskatoon, Canada. I reasoned that the fare would cost far less than a year's schooling and Canada might fire his imagination.

A year later he returned, announcing shortly after his arrival, 'I want to be a doctor.' I gathered that this was mainly due to his brief love affair with the student Rosemarie, which gave him the self-confidence, along with her encouragement, to think about taking up a worthwhile and challenging career.

Delighted but also a little alarmed, I asked doubtfully, 'But Nick do you think you could pass all those awful exams?'

'I think so. But first I want to have the IQ test that you recommended.' He said this with firmness, looking me straight in the eye, his chin belligerent and his whole body poised for battle.

In Canada it seemed IQ tests were normal practice. Another method which had helped Nick lay in their assessing their pupils in an imaginative way; giving high marks for whatever talents the child possessed however outlandish by British standards. Because Nick was a skilled carpenter (he had learnt woodworking while at college in Canada and had made his Aunt Liz a mighty wardrobe), his overall marks were boosted considerably.

'Right,' said I, picking up the phone to speak to Eve, a friend who was a psychologist.

Two days later she rang in great excitement. 'That boy of yours has an IQ of 145. Of course he will be able to study medicine.'

The boost to Nick's confidence was tremendous as he carried like a life line the scrap of paper Eve had given him.

By a stroke of good fortune, I heard of Millfield School and the remarkable Mr. Myer, the Headmaster, who guaranteed a place at university for any student, however great the gaps in their previous education, provided the child had the necessary IQ and was prepared to work really hard. Scraping together every penny, I raised their exorbitant fees and in two years Nick, who had never passed an exam in his life except for O Level English, was able to acquire the necessary qualifications to get into medical school. Nick was then awarded a Lord Kitchener scholarship, which paid for his entire medical training, as long as he agreed to spend at least five years in the Royal Navy. Now in his third year at Bart's he was deeply interested in medicine and following in the Richards family tradition.

I have remained puzzled as to why in 1953 British schools failed to suggest IQ tests for obviously intelligent pupils who had lost their way.

Lu too was now on her chosen path. At eleven, shortly after starting at the local grammar school she had asked in a puzzled way.

'What am I supposed to be doing at this school?'

'Lessons I hope, why?'

'Well,' there was a long pause as she marshalled her thoughts.

'I want to be a dancer but they have nothing to do with dancing at this school so I'm just wasting my time.' She wasn't defiant, just serious and genuinely bewildered.

At her insistence and in total ignorance for I'd no idea of the high standard required, I let her apply for an audition at the Royal Ballet School.

Although she had shown some talent at the local dancing class, obviously enjoying every moment, she had received no classical training whatsoever.

The audition must have been humiliating for her as she was unable to understand the simplest of commands and she was surrounded by ballet-wise children, sprucely equipped to the last sophisticated toe nail and snapping into the correct classical movements. She emerged after this ordeal, her sensitive small face white and drawn, biting back tears. As we waited in the pouring rain for the Hammersmith bus she gazed up at me, big grey eyes pitifully expressive,

'When can I try again Mummy?'

So it hadn't deterred her but simply made her more determined.

I took note, made some enquiries and found a ballet school near London with fees I felt I could afford. Mrs. Mortimer, the formidable headmistress, said they would take her but added,

'As Louanne is almost twelve she is really too old to take up ballet as a career. But here she will be able to continue with her ordinary school work and at the same time gain an appreciation of the arts.

I still hesitated, for Lu seemed too young to be taken at her word, but I had learnt over the years to respect her good sense. We also, I felt, had a special bond for on the day of her birth on 6th May 1941, our lives had almost come to an abrupt end during the Exeter bombing. Having just had a Caesarian, I was unable to be moved with the other patients to the comparative safety of the basement. Lu was placed in her cot under my bed and I was given a tin bowl to protect my head and we were left to manage as best we could. Barely conscious of the nightlong crashes and explosions, I was amazed to be told the next morning that one wing of the hospital and part of the Cathedral had been demolished. My small daughter had endured all this with stoic calm, surely an indication of staunch determination.

I had noticed too that in this one term at Grammar School she, who had always moved as lissome as an otter in a stream, was now hunching her shoulders and looking slack and heavy for one so slim and dainty. If this was an indication of inner conflict then it was time to take note.

Then I had one of my peculiar dreams. I was sitting in the Opera House at Covent Garden with Lu aged about three in my arms all warm and cuddly. Ninette de Valois walked towards us down the centre aisle, held out her arms to Lu who struggled off my lap and ran towards her. I was left with a deep sense of loss. My child had gone from me, but as I watched I could see her radiant happiness as she was held in the arms of the other woman.

All next day I pondered unable to shake off the impression left by this dream, so different from the ordinary dreams, forgotten almost before one wakes. This dream was so compelling, so urgent, remaining dramatically clear as though an inner voice was crying, 'Take note, this is important.'

So telling no one about the dream, but taking it as a pointer, I packed Lu off to Elmhurst, where she worked with grinding determination. Contrary to all expectations, at sixteen she joined the Royal Ballet School and then the Royal Ballet Company. She was now excitedly looking forward to touring America before going on to Russia. So Lu too was independent. I could no longer make either of the children an excuse for this single-minded, basically selfish life that I was leading.

It had been a wonderful experience, but I was becoming increasingly aware of the pointlessness of it all for me personally. I was being driven with no time to think, no time for friends and no time for the children on their brief visits. I was a successful hotelier but as a woman a disaster. If I'd been interested in making a lot of money it would have been different, but it was the satisfaction of doing things well, pleasing people, creating something out of nothing, that gave me contentment. I still had as little skill in handling money as I'd had fourteen years earlier. Perhaps Clifford had been right when he said, 'Women rarely stick at anything.' Was it because of women's dissatisfaction when out of touch with their feelings? Would I now have to claw myself back to a more human way of life? Would the fight never stop I wondered sadly.

Over the next few months I reviewed the fourteen years that lay behind me. There had been my fierce battle to bring up the children in freedom on their own small patch of earth; the long fight to equip the Seagull and then to become established as a worthwhile hotel.

There had also been the anxiety and heartache over Gerdy's departure and the near bankruptcy that followed, plus the more subtle conflict of being a business woman in a man's world. I had never wanted to be thrusting and suspicious, but those fourteen years had taught me that to be gentle and gullible spelt disaster.

Two small incidents sprang to mind – each one had made me that much more cynical

A high gale had blown several slates off the roof. I gave the job to a lively young Irish chap who had recently started up in business. By chance I was looking out of the window when he and his mate arrived. I happened to be putting the car away when two hours later they finished the job. The bill arrived itemizing eight hours work for two men at so much an hour, so many slates at so much each. The total was £38 and it seemed excessive, so I rang my old friend Mr. White.

'How much are the best slates?' I asked. 'What is the top rate of pay per hour for slate layers? Would there be any extra items that ought to be included?'

'Well,' boomed Mr. White. 'You'd have to add time to order the slates, time to get to the job and back, hire of a long ladder if it's a small firm and of course danger money on that windy roof of yours.' He roared with mirth.

'I reckon for that job with the number of slates, if your man quoted £12, it would be about right. High, but fair.'

I tackled my Irish friend as I wrote out a cheque for £12. Not a bit abashed, he laughed holding out his hand.

'Fair enough Mam, no hard feelings I hope. I was only trying it on because you're a woman. I didn't think you'd know about prices and t'ings.'

I shook his wretched hand because he was so disarming, but I was furious. He was treating it all as a game. What a way to do business I thought sullenly.

The second episode irritated me even more for it was conducted on a more professional basis. When our table licence was granted I had submitted plans of The Seagull to the magistrates. After this one brief airing they had remained neatly rolled in a cupboard. Three years later the licence had to be renewed. As the lawyer who had handled the original application had now retired I consulted Mr. Starch, who had been highly recommended as an up and coming young man. The question of plans arose.

'I will get Mr. Duke to draw them up' he said briskly.

'Oh that won't be necessary' I told him. 'I have the original ones which were used last time. There have been no further alterations to the building so they haven't been touched since then. They will be perfectly OK.'

Mr. Starch looked shocked. 'We can't produce old plans in Court, as we have our professional standards to think of you know Mrs. Richards.'

'That may be' I replied, 'But there's nothing to upset anyone's professional pride in the original plans. They've only be used once, haven't been opened up since then, so they are in perfect order. I'm not going to the expense of having new ones drawn. They cost me seven guineas then so they must do.' I stared Mr. Starch straight in the eye.

The licence was renewed and the bill arrived three times greater than the original one. One item stood out as though written in letters of fire. 'To drawing plans of The Seagull, twelve guineas.' Quivering with indignation I rang Mr. Starch pointing out that this was contrary to my instructions, so he would have to pay for the plans himself. He waffled on about his professional dignity being at stake. In the end we decided to submit my complaint to the Law Society. Much to Mr. Starch's surprise he received a carefully worded reprimand. To my chagrin they suggested we ought to split the cost of the plans and as I was too busy at the time to continue with this squalid wrangling, I paid my half, but was convinced Mr. Starch would never have tried this nonsense on with a man.

Angela's visit became a turning point. I knew I must not continue with this self destructive life that left no time for compassion. I realised with piercing clarity that I had to step off the perpetual whirl and look inwards, find my lost self, then put the knowledge I had gained over these hard, though happy, years to more useful purpose.

But to what and how? I would have to earn my living that was certain, for any profit made by The Seagull had all gone on school fees.

A young pretty widow is just tolerable if she hasn't too many dependents or too many problems, but a middle aged widow is everyone's nightmare and I had jogged unheeding into my late forties.

I reviewed with misgiving my widowed aquaintances. The 'jolly' girls clinging to their giddy indiscretions while ignoring the mocking glances of their friends. Timid ladies hiding their aching loneliness in genteel bedsits, whilst playing with voluntary work to fill in time. Frayed women with nerves taut hitting the bottle whilst alienating their teenage sons and daughters. Desperate ladies grateful for attention from any man however unsuitable. I could see myself in none of these uncomfortable roles, but the time for change had come.

Chapter 26

1958 – The End Game

But I still had to sell The Seagull and this proved to be more difficult that I'd anticipated. The agency produced a few prospective buyers but they all cried off at the last moment. He then told me that our excellent reputation, particularly in cooking, had scared them. They feared that they would receive complaints from discontented clients if they could not achieve our high standard. From what I'd seen of them I was inclined to agree.

The trouble was that The Seagull was 'out of context'. It was absolutely right for families, but buyers aiming at our culinary standards knew that the clientele they hoped to attract were not drawn to Exmouth, preferring more exclusive seaside resorts like Budleigh Salterton and Salcombe.

After several months of uncertainty I had to make a decision, and converting the hotel into flats seemed a sensible solution. People were, in the 1950s, beginning to move from large inconvenient houses into self-contained and easily run apartments. The Seagull was ideal for this purpose as it was situated on the edge of the sea.

With very little alteration I found the house could be divided into seven comfortable flats, with two very small flats being suitable for one person only, the other five would be spacious with one or two bedrooms.

I contacted the splendid Mr. Priaux who had made such a success of the dining room conversions several years before. He agreed that it would be a fairly simple matter. When his estimate for £6,300 arrived, I once again contacted the bank as it would mean another loan. I already had two eager buyers willing to pay £3,500 for the two best flats and felt sure I would have no difficulty in finding buyers for the other five, so I approached the new manager with confidence. With all expenses paid I stood to make a profit of roughly £9,000, which would be a good start in whatever new life I chose to follow.

Armed with this hopeful prospect I tackled the new manager, Mr. Teddon, a pedantic man, with an impersonal, pompous manner, a down turned mouth and sombre narrow eyes. He cautiously agreed that conversion was probably the best solution but as the bank would be lending me the £6,300 he insisted categorically that I must employ a fully qualified architect and also a fully qualified agent to sell the flats.

A leaden silence settled on us like a warning of thunder as I was ripped from my complacency.

'But that isn't necessary' I protested. 'Mr. Priaux and I have worked together most happily and successfully in the past. We've drawn up the plans with his draughtsman. He assures me there will be no difficulty in getting them passed by the planning authority. If I employ an architect it will be an unnecessary expense. He will only come between me and Mr. Priaux and his men. An architect is bound to muddle things.'

'Mrs. Richards I'm sorry, it is you who will muddle things if you interfere. You will be far wiser to leave it all in the hands of the experts. I'd advise you to go right away leaving everything to the architect and the agent. In fact, if you insist on supervising the work yourself I don't think Head Office will be happy about

lending you this large sum. Men don't like women interfering.'
He was more pompous than ever.

I was incredulous and protested vigorously,

'But Mr. Teddon on what do you base this advice? You have
only recently arrived. You were not here seven years ago when
the big alterations took place. If you had been you would know
how well everything went, and we didn't have an architect
then. Mr. Priaux and I know every brick, pipe and joist. I
know and like his men, we work well together. I do assure
you that an estate agent isn't necessary either. I've sold two of
the flats already for a good price. I've researched the area and
know I can sell the rest with no difficulty. I shan't even have
to advertise. I plan to camp on the spot moving from flat to
flat furnishing each one simply and comfortably as they are
completed. I promise there will be no problem. In this way I
can keep an eye on everything. You must know how things slip
if the one who is paying isn't around to keep things moving.'

'I'm sorry' said Mr. Teddon starchily. It was all too obvious
that he despised women.

'I insist. If the bank lends you this money you must fall in with
our wishes. I suggest you employ Mr. McNeil as architect, an
excellent man, Mr. Cooper as agent. Both are highly qualified
and will serve you well if you leave them to get on with the job
without interference.'

At this point I should have insisted on meeting the Bank
directors. I should have stood fast and fought, but I was too
exhausted. Those fifteen years of anxious hard work had
whittled away all my energy. I knew that if I did what Mr.
Teddon suggested it would be disastrous, that the alterations
would cost thousands more if I wasn't on the spot, but I gave in.
Almost perversely I thought 'If this is what he wants I'll show

him how idiotic he is. I'll go away and leave them to muddle about and he will see what a hash will be the result'.

What I felt was not a futile resentment but a great big smashing anger boiling under the surface. In fact I was living in a nightmare realising that fears, fights and worries are too heavy a cargo for any one person, that I was too tired to battle any longer for what I knew to be right.

I had boundless faith in myself but none at all in so called 'experts'. I had become cautious, even cynical knowing that 'experts' never learn from their mistakes. They can always find some outlandish reason to account for their own inadequacies and really don't care. This is called being professional, not getting emotionally involved in their client's problems.

By taking Mr. Teddon's advice so supinely, I made the greatest mistake of my life.

I went up to London to look after the daughter of a friend and caretake their beautiful Knightsbridge house, where Lu rented the top flat. I visited The Seagull every two months appalled by the waste, apathy and sheer stupidity of the work. Mr. Priaux had fallen out with Mr. McNeil, considering him a fool, which he was. He had now lost interest as I was no longer there to push them all along. The men were loafing about playing cards, drinking buckets of tea whilst waiting for bricks that failed to arrive. Scaffolding was up for nine expensive weeks completely unused because paint was undelivered. Walls were being put up with inch gaps so had to be pulled down and rebuilt after my complaints to Mr. McNeil who seldom visited the place.

When he did he missed every detail that was going wrong. But far worse, after agreeing with me, Mr. Priaux and Mr. Teddon that £6,300 was a fair price and six months a reasonable time in which to complete the work, Mr. McNeil had then, unknown to me, put everything on a 'cost plus' basis, telling Mr.Priaux that there was no need to worry. He could charge what he liked and take as long as he wished. All our honest relationship and respect for each other had vanished and his final bill came to £12,800. Instead of six months the work took fifteen months to complete.

My lawyer sent down a surveyor from Birmingham who found that all the mistakes and carelessness I'd itemised were correct. He considered I had a case against Mr. Priaux and Mr. McNeil, but warned me.

'If you had £50,000 I'd advise you to take them both to court. I think you'd have a good chance of winning. But you have nothing and however good the case one never knows how things will turn out in a court of law. You could be landed with an enormous bill. I advise you to leave well alone Kirstine.'

I had no choice but to take his advice.

The agent had been equally unhelpful, in fact positively obstructive. He assured me I was asking too much for the remaining five flats although the people to whom I had sold the first two were delighted feeling they had a bargain. After Mr. Cooper had sold the next two at £2,500 instead of the £3,500 I'd planned, I could see bankruptcy ahead if I allowed this to go on. So I moved into each of the last three flats in turn, at once getting the price I'd originally planned by handling the sales myself.

The bank of course got their money back. Mr. Priaux was paid in full. Mr Cooper got his commission on all six flats, although I had sold five of them. Mr. McNeil received £50 out of his bill of £250 with my promise to pay £10 for the next 20 years. In order to keep one tiny flat as a family base I had to borrow £250 from my brother in law.

A sad ending after fifteen years of grinding hard work and a modicum of success. I felt bleak, depressed, disillusioned and uncertain where to turn, but I was free to plan a completely new life.

Penniless but free. Never again I vowed would I put myself in the hands of 'experts'. Then on a dreary winter evening as I huddled disconsolately in my little flat a friend called casually dropping the solution in my lap.

'Would this interest you, I wonder?' she asked as she handed me a letter, 'I don't want to leave Exmouth nor do I want to start training all over again, but you might find it worthwhile.'

The post offered was that of adoption secretary in an adoption agency. It would mean interviewing and assessing prospective adopters, helping unmarried mothers, then piloting babies with their new parents through the probationary period before the adoption order was granted.

The salary was infinitesimal, but to me the interest the job presented far outweighed any hardship. Best of all it offered a professional training. This was it! This was what I had been waiting for. All the months of indecision while considering unsuitable jobs dropped away in an instant.

In this post I should be able to use to the full any skills I possessed. Surely, I mused, the years spent watching families must have given me some insight in assessing potential parents. I knew, who better, the difficulties of an unsupported mother, knew how hard it was bringing children up on one's own, but I also knew it could be done. This knowledge would certainly help when confronted by a youngster torn by indecision.

'If they will take me this is what I want' I told my friend quietly.

So in just a few months I had the immense privilege of becoming in mid-life a quiveringly eager student, timidly carrying a pile of text books into the hallowed portals of Church House, Deans Yard, Westminster.

A new stimulating career was stretching out before me. But that is another story.

§

ABOUT THE AUTHOR

Kirstine Richards née Rassmussen

Kirstine was born in Edinburgh to a Danish father, Christian Rassmussen, and a Scottish mother, Hilda Hill-Jones, on 14th March 1912,

She attended Edinburgh School of Art for one year until her father died and the fees could no longer be paid. Life with her eccentric mother became intolerable. Fortunately an aunt came to the rescue and Kirstine moved to Devon, where she worked as a poorly paid designer at the Honiton Pottery.

Subsequently Kirstine opened a café on Honiton High Street, called the 'Highland Fling'. It served excellent coffee and home made cakes, making it very popular. She met her future husband, Gerald Arthur Richards, a young medical student from St. Bartholomew's Hospital at the 'Highland Fling'.

Their two children, Nicholas and Louanne, were born during the 2nd World War. Their father, Gerry, was accidentally wounded in Burma and died at Imphal on 23rd January 1945, shortly before the end of the war.

Kirstine, now a widow with young children, had to find a way of earning a living. She and Gerdy Ramsay, a German friend, who was also a war widow and mother of two, established a family hotel, 'The Seagull', in Exmouth in Devon. The hotel opened in 1947.

In 1959 Kirstine moved on from being a hotelier to become the case worker at the newly formed Agnostic Adoption Society, which was later to become the Independent Adoption Society.

On retirement, she went to live near her cousin in the South of France, where she rented a small house, paying for her keep by hosting Summer guests. A secondary cancer made her decide to move back to England. She found an apartment at Queen Alexandra's Court in Wimbledon, an attractive establishment for widows of officers who had served in the forces.

Kirstine died at St. Raphael's hospice in London on the 25th February 1989.